ANCESTRY DISCOVERIES

WHAT HAPPENS UNDER THE SHEETS DOESN'T STAY THERE

A MEMOIR

ANCESTRY DISCOVERIES

WHAT HAPPENS UNDER THE SHEETS DOESN'T STAY THERE

A MEMOIR

ANNETTE L. BECKLUND

Dedicated in memory of my parents
Ernie, Alice & Barry

Thanks for having me.

"You own everything that happened to you. Tell your stories. If people wanted you to write warmly about them, they should have behaved better."

—Anne Lamott

Table of Contents

Prelude to Discovery

When you take a recreational DNA test for fun and excitement to discover your complete ethnicity, you never know what you are going to get. Perhaps you might be related to someone famous. Personally, I was hoping for a connection to Lucille Ball or Carol Burnett. Then again, if you are like me, you may be on track for the roller coaster ride of your life. Everywhere I go, someone has either had this experience themselves or has a close friend or family member who found out their dad was not their dad. "Ancestry Discoveries" is about the search for DNA connection, disconnection, and sometimes reconnection. But mostly, this book is about self-connection. It is a survival story, where the protagonist, yours truly, a therapist for over twenty years, chose to be an adventurer, a pioneer, while maintaining a sense of humor rather than choosing to be a victim. I had no choice in how I came to be in this world, but I have a choice in how I choose to navigate through every single day in this amazing, sometimes daunting, always adventurous journey we call life. My DNA discovery is part of this life package whether or not I want it to be. My choice in the matter was nonexistent but I have possibilities like anyone else to curl up in a fetal position or maintain a pioneering spirit while on my journey. I am not alone.

You are not alone. My hope in telling my story is that I can help others find their own voices, to tell their own stories. Telling your story is the way to healing and peace.

According to a study by Dr. Gina Daniel, anywhere between one and thirty percent of the population are MPEs/NPEs—Mis-attributed Parentage Experienced/Not Parent Expected, depending on whose study she quotes. This group comprises late discovery adoptees who were never told they were adopted, and donor conceived individuals (personally, I prefer "artificial insemination" because sperm banks pay the sperm "contributor"). There are the "nobody told me my dad was not my father" or "nobody told me my mom was not my biological mother" individuals, born of extramarital affairs or sexual assault. In summary, a group of people who had a right to know but were never told that they were not biologically connected to someone or to family they believed they were related to. Whatever the circumstances, we all grew up in various decades with different belief systems, diverse cultural world views, socioeconomic backgrounds, religions, and spiritual belief systems and languages. Our perceptions of our experience are as unique as we are. But one thing we all have in common as humans is the need to connect with others and in my case, this need was to unite with my unknown biological family, my kin, my tribe, even if the discovery only led to being able to look into eyes that looked like mine for a minute. I felt this need to connect on a cellular level and the reason was indefinable to me.

There are attachments and there are connections. An attachment is someone who is related to us for some unspecified reason, such as a shared parent or cousin. Connections are individuals that we actually feel a bond or interrelatedness with. My attachments growing up were never quite right, and I attributed this to something I could not identify and something that I causally did wrong. I grew up with adults around me, but not the ones, in retrospect, that I needed. Ironically, my strongest attachment and connection was with the man I called dad for all my life. He was my primary nurturing parent. My mother could not assume that role, probably because she felt guilty and shameful for bearing the child who resulted from an affair to a man she could never have a long-term relationship with. It was not in the cards, nor was it socially acceptable back in the early 1960s to divorce or live out the fantasy of finding someone who filled the need that could not seem to be filled, for a connection that she was not getting from her husband, my dad. This is a deep need for connection that causes someone to stray into another man's arms. I truly believe that my mother was lonely and quite possibly depressed.

Imagine questioning your attachments (or lack thereof) with your primary caregivers your whole life, to finally have the reasons made known. Suddenly, I stopped blaming myself and ceased accepting responsibility for my missing connections. The past four years have progressed from trauma to understanding to acceptance (unless it is Father's Day and I have another meltdown, which has happened more than once). I have most of the answers I need to help me understand the child that I was, who spent years moving from childcare providers to babysitters including biological "sitters" as my mom would call them, but never having the woman whose attention I craved most, who clearly had difficulty forming an early attachment to me. It was not my fault. I was clueless and innocent. I was a child. As you read, you may sense the contradictions in my feelings about the individuals involved in my life. It has been my experience to move from one stage of my grief to another, denial, anger through acceptance and then back to anger again. Stages are fluid. There is no rhyme or reason, it just is. Healing is messy. As a wound heals from the inside out, sometimes, if you are not providing effective wound care (usually caring for yourself), the wounds open and fester, needing to be cleaned to start the healing process all over again.

Health histories of course, are a constant challenge and they are important to preventative care and overall well-being. Ironically, in my case, my dad and my biological father had a lot of similarities. Both had cancer and heart disease. My biological father had a major mental illness and battled with alcoholism which may have contributed to his untimely demise.

Thanks to recreational DNA companies like Ancestry and 23andMe, who have marketing genius on their side, MPEs and NPEs are and will be increasing in number. Originally, I had planned on having this book published under a pseudonym to protect my privacy. If I was making the choice to disown the secrets and shame attached to my experience, hiding behind an assumed name did not make sense anymore. It was only after Ancestry Discoveries was finished about six months ago and on its way to a round of edits, that I decided to author this book about my DNA story using my legal name. It is, after all, my story. What kind of therapist would I be if I did not follow my own advice? Telling my story offers me the freedom to accept and learn from my experiences, as well as providing an example to the brave and wonderful individuals I work with in the sacred space of therapy. Nevertheless, the name Alexandra A. Barrie is a symbolic name I have been blogging with since 2019 (and felt comfortable using here). Alexandra is my mother's birth name, Barry is my biological father's name, and A in the middle is me, Annette.

My parents, named Lou and Irene in the pages ahead, were wonderful people. I thank God every day that they were the parents who raised me. As one of my aunts told me in the beginning, "You were loved." My aunt was correct. In spite of my tumultuous beginnings, I was loved.

I spend my days listening to the stories of others, encouraging them to share their pain and trepidations with me and significant members of their world. Now, I have followed my own advice. It is my turn, and this is my story. I own every single bit of it. The names have all been changed, but the content is my truth. If you find yourself relating to one character in particular, pay attention and acknowledge those feelings. It may mean it would help you if you sought therapy and support groups or apologized to a loved one for telling them to "get over it; the past is in the past." If you are an NPE (Not Parent Expected), I hope you find validation and courage to tell your own story. If we know each other and you sense a character is about you and you feel you were negatively misrepresented, then perhaps you should have been a little kinder. I apologize in advance, kinda, sorta, well, not really. Forgiveness is a process, not a one time action. I would have nothing negative to say if I perceived your behavior was kind and supportive rather than self-protective and self-serving. Besides, Mr. or Ms. Feeling Misrepresented, in spite of what you may believe I still love you, but this story is not about you.

1
——

THE RABBIT DIED

"Your children make it impossible to regret your past. They're its finest fruits. Sometimes, the only ones."
—Anna Quindlen

Irene snuffed out her Salem with her "pretty in pink" lipstick imprinted on the filter and dropped it into the silver Pan American Airlines ashtray on her desk. "Shit," she whispered as she slammed down the phone, the sound reverberating through the empty office. "There goes the next eighteen years of our lives," Irene thought. More whispered expletives followed that realization. How would she tell Lou? "Shit, shit, shit!" There was something about the percussive in the word that soothed Irene. Truly, she loved to curse. It wasn't proper for a lady to curse; however, she was alone in the office. The brief pleasure of the repeated expletive was soon over. All Irene felt was dread, sudden and heavy in the pit of her stomach like an atomic bomb, a stomach that would not be flat for long. "It couldn't be Frank's," she muttered aloud, though she knew deep down that it was. After their usual battle of Lou complaining that Irene was not home much anymore, Lou and Irene had had the best makeup sex they had ever had three weeks ago. Irene seduced Lou and felt assured that if her extra-marital encounter led to pregnancy, she could pass the baby off as her husband's without question. She never dreamed her intentions would actually culminate in pregnancy.

Later that day, after receiving the phone call from Irene, Lou danced his way home from the office on cloud nine. "Another baby!" he shouted to the sky. "Woohoo!" Lou was proud of his accomplishments. Five babies and he had barely turned forty-five. He came from a family of nine and he was hoping for another young strapping lad to keep the Pedersen family name going. Three daughters and one son were nice, but he would really love another son.

Maybe he and Irene were headed in the right direction after all. Maybe Irene would be staying home a little more often and stop working so late. Lou had his suspicions about Irene in the past. She worked way too many late nights claiming she had to "finish up" and had "work related dinners" too many times. The handsome ingrate he found in his home several weeks ago with Irene after he returned home from bowling was never coming back. Lou made sure of that.

Lou maintained his blind faith regarding his relationship with his wife and believed Irene would never cheat on him. He preferred denial. Off Lou went with a lilt in his walk, detouring his trek home from work to visit his in-laws, who already had a shot and a beer ready to celebrate whatever he had to tell them. Lou loved his in-laws. It wasn't that long ago he was living downstairs renting their tiny apartment with their daughter and the four kids. He adored his mother-in-law especially. She was kind, considerate, loving, and she had bright blue eyes and a body like a little refrigerator. His own mother didn't care too much for Irene. She was somewhat distant at times. Irene used to say it was because her husband was a secondary breadwinner in the family and Grandma Pedersen resented Irene for being the reason Lou left home, *finally, at the age of twenty-five to get married. After walking the mile to visit Bertha and Joe, Lou stopped in to tell their neighbor—his good friend Michael Delancey— the news. By the time he got home that evening, he had a plate of pasta to warm up for Irene and he was high as a kite on whiskey and life.*

Irene, on the other hand, had already bolted into the bathroom for the fourth time that day. Up came her lunch. This was it, she thought to herself, looking down at the multi-colored, putrid smelling chunks. This was her punishment. She was disgusted with herself, disenchanted with life, and depressed as hell. She knew the truth. These are things a woman knows.

Years ago, I wrote the story of my conception along with my mother's pregnancy to show the contrasting feelings my parents had about me coming into the world as a "surprise" child, the midlife crisis baby, the "oopsie." Based purely on personality along with my relationship with each of my parents, I guessed my mother had negative feelings while my dad was probably thrilled. That is what I believed. I was working through my childhood issues at the time and was forewarned by another therapist not to write about my conception. "It could bring up conflicting feelings for you, Alexandra." My inner child was wounded, and she needed attention. Little Alexandra, my inner child who felt like she was around seven years old, needed nurturing. I searched for reasons as to why I was reading my mother the way I was. As an adult, my mom and I had a loving relationship. However, as a child, I never understood her lack of maternal connection. It was sometimes difficult and it made me sad to think about it. The puzzling feelings were there and I couldn't ignore them. On some level, in the eyes and heart of the child that I was, I thought I did something wrong. I had difficulty reconciling my earlier relationship with my mom. After my mother's death, I decided it was time to search deeper within myself for the reasons why

I believed I had done something harmful to cause her pain. My therapist and I even sat for several sessions, trying to figure out what my mother's diagnosis might have been. We always came up empty. I knew my mother was depressed based on some of her erratic behavior and the songs she would sing when nobody was around except for me. She would talk to herself in unintelligible syllables and sang "The Prisoner Song." I can still hear her voice in the back of my head. Irene always had a flare for drama. "Oh I wish I had someone to love me."

When I took the time to reflect on my emergence into life, it was easy to empathize with my beautiful career-minded mother who was in her prime and what she might have felt finding out she was pushing out another infant at age forty-two, ten years after her last child was born. I had compassion for her having wee ones out of diapers with the freedom that brings and suddenly starting all over again with no sleep, baby formula and potty training. It was my decision to change the narrative once I discovered two weeks after my fifty-seventh birthday that my dad, who I have worshipped for all my life, was not my biological father. One of the first people I called was my therapist. I had not spoken to her in some time, but I wanted her to know the great mystery of what to diagnose Irene with was solved. Irene did not have a diagnosis. My mother carried that guilt and shame throughout my existence, living with a secret she kept from me and took to her grave. Irene built a wall around herself in my early years to shield herself from the pain and humiliation she must have felt.

Looking back now, my essay written so long ago was a foreshadowing of what was to come. On a positive note, everything has now come full circle, and I am gifted with the knowledge of why my mother was distant in my early years. My mother was upset that I was coming into existence at her age of forty-two, not because of her age, but because I was a child from an office love affair. I am a member of a "club that nobody wants to belong to," and in my case, wish I wasn't writing from personal experience about NPEs (Not Parent Expected) or MPEs (Mis-attributed Parentage Experience). In the support groups for those like me with mis-attributed parentage, we have affectionately referred to ourselves as a "club." This NPE phenomenon brought on by people like me who embark on recreational DNA testing feeling it will be fun but finding ourselves in a state of shock and trauma has become more common thanks to companies like Ancestry, 23andMe and My Heritage to name only a few. Those of us in this unpopular club were left with the unexpected mystery of deciphering where we came from and what clandestine surprises lay before us in the land of unexplored health histories. Just when we thought we had the answers, this twist of fate changed all the questions. Many of our parents are deceased and some, like mine, appeared to have kept the information guarded under lock and key, only to be shared with individuals possessing security clearance that transcends the Pentagon's. I knew who I was; I thought. I knew my heritage; I thought. I gave health histories to many physicians and insurance companies; I thought I knew that too. But alas, all those years with all that information on which paternal diseases I might inherit or pass along through the genes, was completely wrong.

My desire at fifty-six, just before my birthday when I first embarked on this journey, was to have fun and to learn more about my roots. Let's face it, you can buy a DNA test for under $100. "It makes a splendid gift," says the advertisement, flooding social media and commercial television. The carefully sculpted advertisements lightheartedly warned me, "You may discover you have to trade in your kilt for lederhosen or find relatives from the Mayflower!" In my case, break out the shofar! Cook up the spaghetti! Dispose of those Swedish meatballs. What was supposed to be "fun" and "entertaining" turned out to be a traumatic experience for me, like so many thousands of others.

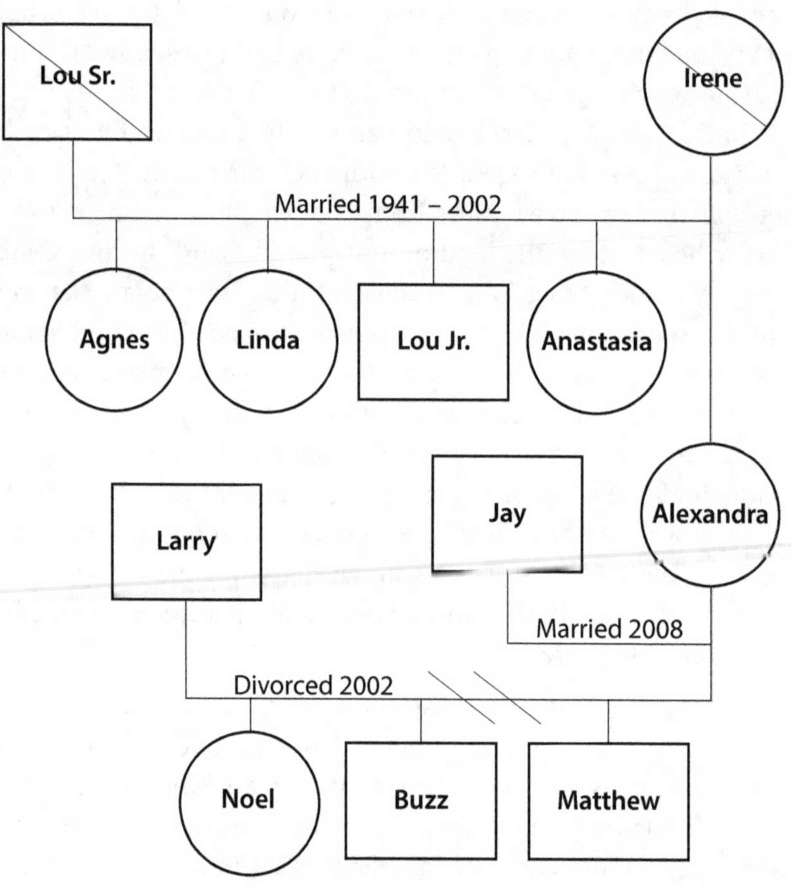

Alexandra's Original Family
Prior to Discovery

I am the youngest of five in my "original" family. My siblings are referred to as my "originals." The eldest, Agnes, is eighteen years older than I am. My mother dubbed her "second mother." I grew up buying into that silly myth at first. Agnes seemed to buy into it when it was convenient for her. I loved the way she mommied her own kids. She was the type of mom who taught her kids how to take care of themselves in the morning. Agnes was well organized, tidy, and she looked like Doris Day. Cereal boxes were placed in convenient cabinets to satisfy the early morning risers' little tummies. Of course, having easy pour Tupperware cereal containers and milk stored on the lower shelves within reach for little kiddies, allowed the adults in the household to sleep in for a few extra minutes. I slept over at Agnes' home while my parents traveled. There were planned activities to keep everyone busy and make them tired so they would go to bed, sometimes while the sun was still out. My nieces and nephews were close in age, and I loved spending time at Agnes' home. It was structured fun and structure in my life was severely lacking. I vowed that I, too, would be a mom like Agnes when it came time for me. Agnes was present. Unlike my mother, Agnes did not work outside the home. My nieces and nephew were not latchkey kids like me.

Thanks to Agnes, I have a niece and nephew close in age to me who have become friends in our adult life. I still love Agnes to this day as she is part of my history, and she is my half-sister. It was what transpired in our adult lives which caused me to lose trust and not appreciate Agnes' actions. There was too much backbiting in the days when my parents became aged and needed care, with Linda, my sister who followed Agnes in birth order, leading the way. Agnes stood by and let it happen. Keeping a secret about my birth father for several years before I spit in the test tube was the final straw. When Agnes was called out on it, she backpedaled saying she didn't know anything. I suppose she forgot what she told me. The good news is my back has recovered from the teeth marks from all that backbiting. When you forgive, you do not have to keep going back for more. Agnes kept the DNA secret from me because it affected Agnes too much, from what I heard. Poor, poor Agnes, always suffering from the pain others are feeling. Agnes disclosed because, "I didn't want to take this secret to my grave." I am still laboring over forgiveness, and I have found forgiveness to be a challenging but necessary part of my process.

My mother dubbed Agnes with the "second mother" title, something she did not want and I ultimately rejected, even more so now that the truth has been brought to light. We were not connected. We were attached because of our shared parentage.

Linda is the second-born child in my original family. She is sixteen years older than I am. There is only one word for Linda that resonates throughout the entire time I have known her: nasty. Linda is mean. She never liked me. Linda did one kind big sisterly thing that I can remember. She baked cupcakes for my first-grade class when I turned seven. I hold on to that memory when I look for something positive to recall about Linda to minimize any negative feelings I still harbor. I don't think about her much anymore unless my nephew brings her up in conversation.

During my time in therapy, I recalled an event that happened when I was three years old. Linda was making pudding on the stove. The three-year-old me overturned a tray of bowls filled with boiling hot pudding that Linda left too close to the end of the table. The pudding, too hot to eat, came pouring down on my chest. My shirt had to be peeled off, along with my skin, and I was immediately hoisted into the sink and submerged in cold water. I made the mistake of attempting to verify this event with Agnes. Agnes' voice became high pitched, and I had to endure hearing how the event made her feel.

I have no recollection of the pudding event. I needed details so that I could put the feeling to rest that Linda's hot pudding on the toddler accident was not purposeful. When you do not know the full truth, you fill in your own missing details with imagination. Based on the behaviors I witnessed and endured from Linda throughout my life, I presumed the worst. Unfortunately, Linda was never held accountable for her behaviors. I am told my mother usually said Linda couldn't clean because she had astigmatism. Her abuse of her younger sister was never called out that I can remember. My mother's excuse was "People have cruel behavior because they probably have a stomachache." Apparently, Linda had perpetual intestinal issues as I witnessed her abuse one of her kids, singling him out, calling him names, and screaming bloody murder. My nephew and I are seven years apart. When I was around to witness Linda's abuse to her child, I yelled back. Hence my nickname from Linda, "the Mouth", followed.

Once, when Linda was at our home with her kids in the afternoon, and I wouldn't obey her command, she told me I could not eat dinner. Linda was a crappy cook anyway, but I was not about to be on her list of subservient peons. She had kids and a husband to serve that purpose now. I called our dad, and he overturned her tyranny. Linda worshipped my dad. We all did. I am pretty sure she probably felt as though she were about to receive a spanking. As adults, Linda was an armchair quarterback, as the wasband (term I sarcastically use to refer to my former husband), kids and I, were taking care of my parents as they aged. She was nonexistent, judgmental, and blinded by her own hate for me. That's how I see it, at least. I mention her here since she is part of the originals. I thought I forgave her and let her go a long time ago. When you are writing your story, all the angst, all the malice of the past, all the horrid memories resurface. I am forced to forgive and let go yet another time. Letting go is no simple task, but Linda and I haven't spoken in many years. From what I have heard from her adult kids, she still harbors a great deal of hatred towards me. I have green eyes. Linda has green eyes. The likelihood that a green-eyed child with the eye color my mom and dad had is 0 to16%, depending on who is quoting statistics. I don't think she belongs to the gene pool my dad left behind, either.

Lou Jr. is next in line in my originals. I don't remember him in my early years. Mostly, he had his head underneath the hood of a car. He studied mechanics in high school. Lou Jr. had a little black Fiat with a peace sign spray painted on top of it. Lou Jr.'s mechanics left a remnant of grease in our driveway for years. Having that grease spot dissipate over time was the melancholy signal for my parents that Lou Jr. wasn't coming home again. Lou Jr. told me he couldn't wait to leave home. He joined the Navy during the Vietnam era. When he was on leave, he would take me to the bakery after school, and we would indulge in sweets, sugar-coated brownies, and other tasty treats. Lou Jr. taught me how to have a sweet tooth. He was an alright kind of guy to most, with a pleasant personality. When I was a kid, he used to tell me his woes about growing up as the only boy in a female realm and how he was mistreated, being forced to do Linda's chores. Because I was so young, it wasn't until later on and after my own experiences with everyone feeling sorry for Linda, that I could have some semblance of comprehension for what he meant.

As adults, the originals seem to be close and Lou Jr. clings to his three sisters. They have frequent sibling reunions. No, I am not included, and I probably wouldn't go. I remember feeling sorry for my big brother. I was in high school when he abruptly moved, telling no one where he was going, including his wife.

Lou Jr. eventually reached out to my parents again after he settled into Arizona life. It felt like it took forever to hear from him, and we all had to endure my mother's depression and worry. Lou Jr. appeared to rely on the passing of time to dispel any negative feelings anyone might be harboring. Like the rest of my family, he didn't like to talk about anything that even hinted at conflict. As a result, nothing seemed to ever be settled. Some of us made visits and met his second wife. Lou Jr. took us to touristy places like the Grand Canyon and Organ Stop Pizza (my favorite because I play the organ), and the roller skating rink. Lou Jr. broke my parents' hearts by leaving so abruptly, without explanation.

He later said it was because his marriage was over. Of course, it would have been nice for Lou to give his mother the heads-up, but that might have caused a confrontation. My sister, Anastasia, said more than once that our mother stayed alive in a coma longer than she needed to because she was waiting for Lou Jr. to come. I have wondered over the past few years if this were the case or if she had a secret she harbored that kept her on the earth in a coma, something like: your dad is not your father.

Anastasia is next in line. She is ten years older than I am. Anastasia was my favorite sister at one time, and I aspired to be just like her. She was "the attractive one." She was also a smart cookie. Anastasia had her share of gentleman callers. We shared a room while I was growing up. I used to love watching her put her makeup on in the morning. She taught me to love the Beatles and Motown. Anastasia was a sharp, trendy dresser. If she grew her hair long, I had to have my hair long too. As a young adult, Anastasia taught me to cook Italian food because Anastasia had an innate affinity for bad boys and sometimes that included Italian men involved in, ahem, business syndicates. She was a shrewd businesswoman herself. Growing up, I had a blind faith admiration for Anastasia, despite being told when she babysat that I would be tied to a gravestone in chains if I didn't behave. As adults, we spent hours on the phone. Anastasia had a boyfriend who abused her son, my nephew, ten years younger than me. Come to think of it, he abused a lot of us. I couldn't fight the boyfriend off. I tried! I was eighteen and he had me pinned on her kitchen floor, threatening to "deflower" me. Anastasia stood by silently and watched. Anastasia endured her own abuse from him, complete with black and blue bruises. She married him anyway. They divorced after he had a long-term affair with her best friend. Anastasia grew a mustache by accident. Menopause does that to some women. I have chin hairs; Anastasia has a mustache.

Each of us has a unique path to take in this life. Sometimes we walk the path together with others, and sometimes we stumble on our own. I like to believe that everything happens for a reason. Sometimes the reason is "you're stupid and you make poor choices." I try to bear no ill feelings anymore. I view my originals as attachments and not connections. My new reality has caused me an enormous amount of pain, regret, doubt, and mistrust. After all, if you can't trust your own parents, who can you trust? I had to detach and set strict boundaries to preserve my own mental health. Tending to the feelings of others took up so much of my time in my work, that I needed to distance myself from my originals to preserve my own sanity.

Discovering you are an NPE affects the original family and the new family. In my case, I have "original siblings" to consider and "my new family" who were all as shocked as I was. Some were sympathetic and kind such as my maternal and paternal cousins, my new sister, and my new aunts. One was as cold as ever (Linda). Anastasia and Agnes had their doubts about my dad a few years before I found out. They kept it a secret. But where there are secrets, there is shame. This DNA discovery is a shame that strikes the unsuspecting innocents. It is a shame we have a choice to own or disavow. In my family of origin, as I am navigating this experience, the relationship with my original siblings deteriorated to the lowest level it could go. It sounds strange, but I was relieved that my dad died before my mom. He left everything to her when he died. It crossed my mind that if my mom died first, my siblings might try to sue me for any inheritance I had received. I cut off my originals, for good this time.

This DNA discovery made me feel like my whole life was one big fat lie. It drove my siblings and I further apart. I always trusted my parents, and now that wasn't an option anymore. I trusted my originals less. I broke free. This time, the wedge was cemented in with pain, dishonesty, mistrust, and yes, the paradox: love. That love was for me. My attachments could be severed, as what I really wanted my whole life was a connection. The time came to throw in the towel on making the relationships work that I struggled with for most of my life. It is not defeat; it is a realization of sorts. It doesn't matter if I am not invited to their sibling reunions, and it doesn't hurt anymore when the relatives comment about the pictures they post on social media. Coming to the acceptance stage of my grief in detaching from this original set of siblings helped me begin the process of letting go and creating my renewed self, the one who explores and celebrates culture and has the opportunity to connect to a new sister.

After my DNA discovery, I looked for support and acceptance and found none in my original siblings. My expectation was unrealistic when I came from a place of being the oddball. Of course, I never fit in with them anyway and was usually described as "different." I looked different, and I acted different. Different in my original sibling world is unwelcome. The name "spoiled brat" was catapulted my way for a long time. It's okay, I don't get them either. As this DNA discovery reared its head four years ago, I now understand why at least.

When I have felt sad about what would've–could've been, like the genetic mirroring which was sadly missing my whole life, like knowing my new sister and brother and aunts and cousins, I remind myself that they are half siblings and not full siblings. I am not alone here. It's my way of coping. Many of my NPE fellow associates have identified a lack of connection with their original families. How do you rationally define the irrational feelings attached to this? It is hard to say. Healing from a DNA discovery like mine is messy. Healing from any trauma is not linear; it is something you learn to live with. There are not a lot of books written about the experience yet. I hope as you read my story, you do not feel alone. If you are not a member of our undesirable "club of misfit toys," my hope is you may gain some insight and compassion. Our world was turned upside down and inside out. In my case, in the last half of my life. I thought I had finished with my identity crisis a long time ago.

I recognized that I needed help beyond what my husband and

adult kids could offer. I needed people like me, who took recreational DNA tests and had their worlds turned inside out. I found several groups through social media. What I have found through being involved in several NPE support groups online is that there are many of us navigating this experience. Some of my compadres are lucky enough to have supportive siblings from their family of origin. But so many of us are the "odd man out" or the "black sheep" of the family. I like to believe I am the psychedelic one instead, a unique and colorful, creative soul. We are the child in the family who does not fit in. Often it is because we look or act differently. Finding out your dad was not your father, as traumatic as that was, helped me to make sense of the behavior of persons around me while I was growing up. Everything feels like it has come full circle. As I have uncovered my truths, I have embraced a profound forgiveness for my mom. That is a gift.

Another common feature NPEs seem to share is that we grow up minus the genetic mirroring (where we do not look like anyone). It may seem inconsequential to you if you have not experienced this, but to me and my fellow NPEs, finding that connection with someone who you finally look like, is a profound moment in time. You suddenly realize you are not the weird one your family made you out to be. You are unique, original, and perfectly you.

The Right to Know Organization says that if you don't know why you do not look like anyone, "you grow up feeling like something is wrong with you." This resonates with me and so many other NPEs, Donor Conceived (DC) and Late Discovery Adoption individuals. I was ecstatic when my first child bore a resemblance to me. My parents arrived at the hospital to greet their new granddaughter. My dad asked, "Which one is she?" I was beyond elated to point out that she was the one who looked like me as a baby. And she really did. It seems shallow, but I realize now that it doesn't mean something until it really means something. This little being was the first person in my life who looked like me. It affected me on a cellular level. I studied each feature of every relative I grew up with, trying to find a resemblance. I even made concessions with my dad's sister, who had curly dark hair like I do. She was a nun, but that didn't seem to matter. Maybe, I thought for a second, I looked like her or my niece, with dark hair and lighter eyes. Anyone I asked about this, (i.e., "Don't I look like dad's sister Sandy?") would give me a halfhearted answer, which felt more like they were placating me. There are pictures of my dad and me where folks have told us we look alike. "You have your dad's smile." I had many of his mannerisms because growing up as a child, I was Velcroed to my dad's side. We were buddies. Recently, a friend shared with me that she was jealous of the relationship I had with my father.

When you are navigating through this experience of DNA discovery, there is always some well-meaning person who will tell you that "this experience will make you a better person, or mother, or therapist." Usually, they tell you this when you're at the height of feeling like you would like to jump off the nearest bridge. I usually want to tell them to go to hell, but I don't. Someday, I hope I can make light of all of this. I would like to develop a stand-up comedy routine and call it, "MPE Mania." Picture it, me on stage with my opening song, guitar in hand, sitting on a stool singing, "I Am a Mashugana Klutz." I can follow it up with "Dumb things people say to NPEs." The fact is, people say things to me all the time trying to make the negative feelings disappear. They want to fix what they sadly cannot fix. It is well intentioned, but empathy works better than platitudes. Platitudes are well intentioned but leave the recipient feeling invisible.

And here I am, sixty plus years old, left with many questions that will remain in the category of mystery. This is a journey that will continue. You may get through this experience if you are an NPE, but you will never get over it. There is unfamiliar territory to explore, such as new family, recently discovered but unknown health history, and how to handle yourself gracefully when someone asks you about any part of your past now that everything has changed. At the outset, I told anyone who would listen to me about this experience and it entertained wide-eyed grocery workers at the corner market, left co-workers at a complete loss for words, brought out the best in people's compassion, and the worst in others. I went from feeling like I lost my dad all over again, to intense anger with my mother, to forgiveness. I have moved beyond Agnes, Linda, Lou Jr., and Anastasia. On a positive note, I gained a whole new tribe and a culture I continue to process, explore, and assign meaning to. I continue to work on reconciling my past with my present circumstance. The journey trudges forward as my story continues to unfold.

2

BROKEN AND SAD

*"In the midst of winter, I found there was, within me,
an invincible summer."*

—Albert Camus

My husband Jay, my friend Jeannie and I, took a trip to Hawaii in January, 2018. While in Hawaii, Jeannie received an email from her brother informing her they had a sister! Apparently, Jeannie's father had an affair with a woman prior to meeting Jeannie's mother. The result was a sister that he never mentioned or apparently knew anything about. Jeannie seemed beyond shocked and asked me if I would go to the other side of Florida with her when we returned home so she could meet this long-lost sister. Jeannie's sister did an Ancestry DNA test and discovered a first cousin who was also a first cousin to Jeannie and her brother. The new sister contacted the first cousin and discovered she had a half-brother and half-sister, Jeannie and her brother. Adoptees often search for parents and often times discover bonus siblings. Jeannie is a lot less dramatic than yours truly, but this new information seemed to completely blindside her. Her brother is a man of few words or explanations, so Jeannie was left to figure out the mystery on her own. Jeannie had just lost her wife a few months earlier. My family and I were immediately suspicious that this woman could be a fortune hunter of sorts, so I agreed wholeheartedly to join Jeannie when we returned. No gold digger was going to stake a claim on my best friend.

There was no denial that Jeannie and her long-lost sister shared genetic similarities. It was downright uncanny. They looked alike, were the same height, walked alike, and had the same sense of humor. Jeannie and her new sister were pretty close to being identical twins. "Oh my God, there are two of them!" You really didn't need a DNA test to prove anything, but the conversation turned to the recent state of consumer testing options. Two of us vowed to purchase our own tests when we got home. I wanted to be in on all the fun. Who knows what lucky long-lost relatives are out there waiting for me to surface? I joked about it. I announced maybe I would get lucky and find a new sister. Jeannie joked back, laughing hard at her own joke before she got the words out, "It would be a welcomed surprise since your sisters suck." We laughed and laughed. Be careful what you wish for.

In no time at all and several weeks before my fifty-seventh birthday, my Ancestry Discovery kit arrived in the mail. I was so excited about beginning a new adventure! On the very day that Ancestry kit arrived in the mail, I followed the instructions to the letter and managed enough saliva to reach the little marker on the test tube. I activated the kit, sealed it, and off in the mail it went. I received an email that the kit arrived safely. Soon, I could track the changes and whereabouts of my genetic predispositions, ethnicity, and historical attachments. My extended family who also took a DNA test, would meet me on the other side of this adventure once my results have been analyzed in the lab. It was an edgy and exciting time. As soon as my results confirmed how Swedish I was, I would make plans for us to travel to Scandinavia. Jay's dad was Norwegian and mine Swedish, so we could take a cruise or an extensive tour tracking down family. On another trip, we could go to Canada and connect with my French-Canadian relatives. Because we love to travel, it was fun to map out travel plans in my head for the next few years, hoping to connect to some of my dad's family and see parts of the world we had never explored.

My paternal cousin, the self-proclaimed family historian, told me we had northern Native American blood and that our ancestors migrated to Canada. NPEs are often specifically looking for this ethnic trait for whatever reason. I was overly excited to hear this. Maybe I was cosmically connected to ancient ancestors who once roamed the plains. I loved visiting the Crazy Horse monument back in the 80s. I believed it was kismet. Our home and my office had pictures of Sedona, Arizona and our family room was decorated in the motif of all things Native American. The excitement on that fateful day pumped my adrenaline through every atom of my being. My wait was over. Ancestry even said so in an email.

I was eager to sign in and had so much enthusiasm that I could not contain the excitement I felt. "Finally!" I had waited over three weeks for this moment. I downloaded the Ancestry application on my phone. I signed in. The first thing I looked for was "My DNA story" which outlined my ethnicity estimate. This varies as it can change slightly based on science and updates to DNA technology. It also varies one or two percentage points by company. Eastern Europe and Russia are number one. This includes Czech Republic, Slovakia, Poland, and Lithuania. There were no surprises here. I was raised in the Polish culture because it was part of my mother's background. I knew my maternal grandmother had Lithuanian roots even though she was born in Pennsylvania. I was completely confused now. I am European Jewish from the same area of the world that includes Ukraine, Moldova, Eastern Romania, Poland, Slovakia, Hungary, and Moravia. "I am 32% Jewish!" Maybe my grandfather, who was born in Poland, actually had Russian Jewish roots or Polish Jewish roots! Before looking at the rest, I called Anastasia. At the time, we spoke occasionally, every few months, but I had to tell someone, anyone, who might care. I was beyond ecstatic to let her know of our newfound Judaism.

I told her about my findings and that I was still looking. I couldn't believe we had Jewish blood! Now, through all of this, my realization of what exactly was going on was not clear at all. I was excited about finding out that one of my grandparents was Jewish. Anastasia and her husband were both prejudiced towards Jewish people and people of color. I wasn't raised that way, so I am not sure where that came from. I thought I would let her sit with that. I hung up and continued exploring some more heritage. Down the list of percentages of ethnicities I went. I saw absolutely no French and absolutely no Swedish on my list. Native American was noticeably absent. I saw the Baltics mentioned, and I was blown away by Southern Italy, specifically Sicily and northern Italy, and less than 1% from Malta. I was completely frozen in time. I was in shock. Somebody at Ancestry had to have made a mistake. I called Anastasia back, and I was searching for words before allowing myself to panic. I told her about our Italian heritage. She said nothing. I was in shock because apparently, I was not ready to be out of my head or my heart space just yet. My denial defense mechanism was working on overdrive. My defenses were warring with reality and were neck and neck racing around the track. Reality moved closer to the finish line. With great trepidation, I hit the "Alexandra's Matches" button on my Ancestry App. I was breathing heavy and close to hyperventilation.

A sigh of relief hit me as I saw my mom's nieces and nephews, complete with family trees for me to explore. I was searching for the paternal self-proclaimed family genealogist who was probably the first one to line up when these recreational tests became available, and terror hit me in my core. I did not see her name. I didn't see anyone's name I recognized from my dad's family. I spotted a third cousin named Luigi. I was beside myself. I knew something was wrong, horribly wrong. This was a horrendous mistake, and somebody needed to pay for making me feel so awful. This feeling was beyond any rug being pulled out from under me. It was more like I was falling into an abyss of darkness and despair. Minutes felt like lifetimes. I was sweating, I was shaky, I was scared. I called customer service at Ancestry. A very kind voice answered the phone. I told the kind voice my predicament and explained that I was wondering if there were errors made in the DNA laboratory. I was crying now. I couldn't help it. I abandoned all sense of reason. Kindly Mr. Ancestry man told me I should contact Luigi, who was clearly on the screen I was looking at on my iPad. Mr. Ancestry man must have been able to see what I was looking at. I think he told me how to do it, but I sobbed uncontrollably at him on the phone.

"Are you telling me that my dad, the man who raised me, is not my father?" Surely that is a call no person should ever have to make to customer service, and I would bet every customer service person on the other end of the line dreads those calls. He gently suggested again that I reach out to Cousin Luigi to uncover the truth. The following was what I wanted to write:

Dear Cousin Luigi,

Who are you and why am I Italian? And Jewish?

I did not know what to write. For once in my life, I was at a complete loss for words. I wrote the following on that day:

Dear Luigi,

I hope you are well. I just received results from my DNA test and according to Ancestry, we are related. I am more curious than I can tell you and have a zillion questions in mind. I'm 57, from NJ but live in Florida now. My email is AlexandraABarrie@gmail.com Wow. That's all I can say as I am hoping some of the first cousins I have known my whole life show up on my DNA list. My mom and dad are both deceased.

I can only wonder what poor ol' Cousin Luigi must have felt reading that message. Do men fear that they have long-lost children? If it could happen to me, it could happen to him, too. Maybe that's why Cousin Luigi never answered my message. Maybe he thought I was nuts. Continuing my quest, I went down the list of Italian names on my cousins' list. There's Lorenzo, who was next. I had no shame. I wanted answers. I was desperate for the truth. I wrote to him that day too:

Hi Lorenzo,

I just received DNA results from Ancestry, and it would appear we are related. I think I sent a disjointed email to someone in your family – possibly because I'm in shock. So, now I'm just searching for answers. I'm 57 from NJ and now live in Florida. My mom and dad are deceased. Nobody from my dad's family has shown up in my DNA nor has the ethnicity I always thought I inherited from him. I hope we can talk at some point.

Thank you and kindest regards,
Alexandra (AlexandraABarrie@gmail.com)

I guess I was thinking if I kept asking, someone was bound to answer me. I can't imagine what it would be like to get a message like either of the ones I sent. The compassionate, empathetic part of me shut down. I did not care what anyone thought. They probably thought that I was out of my mind. I was in a traumatic state of panic and sadness, and yes, completely out of my mind. I felt like I lost a part of myself that day.

I contacted a paternal cousin to ask her if the family genealogist had her DNA test done, still trying to rule out mistakes. She said that yes, her sister did indeed take the test and was planning a trip to Canada with her granddaughter to visit the French-Canadian relatives.

I needed grounding; it was urgent. I needed someone to tell me I was still their sister, that I was still a part of our family, that my life was not a lie. I felt helpless and out of control, so I made the mistake of calling Anastasia back and her husband answered. He made fun of us because we are Jewish. The irritation caused me to tell a lie. I told him we were African, too. Maybe that would shut him down. He apparently teased Anastasia about being African after that phone call and she denied the African heritage, and he said very point blank, "Alexandra wouldn't lie to me." Well, if everyone else was lying, perhaps it was my turn. By this time, I was beyond upset and I begged my sister to please get a DNA test done. At the time of writing, Anastasia did not get her DNA tested. Luigi and Lorenzo never answered me back. I have cowards on both sides of my family.

So began the struggle, which felt like a race to see who would win the Alexandra sperm donor prize. I did not have a plan, but I needed one. I functioned on lack of sleep, coffee, and a dining room table that contained drawings, names, and lists of suppositions. The next two weeks were filled with battling inner demons, anger, depression, uncertainty, and boundless anxiety attacks. I don't remember how I worked or functioned. Operating on automatic pilot became second nature. I maintained my therapy practice and consulted at the hospital. In the beginning, I called my biological father "sperm donor" because I was angry. I was a mere shell of who I was, and there were days when I wanted to die. My soul seemed irrevocably injured.

I went to work, I came home. I had no idea how my obsession with finding out the truth affected anyone. I asked no one, which is not like me at all. Usually, I worry how everyone else will feel. Respond, don't react; screw that. I didn't care. I wanted to know who I was and where I came from. I wanted to connect with my kin. I wanted to open my eyes and wake up from a nightmare. I longed for the day when the inner screaming and crying I endured would finally stop. My soul longed for the missing pieces that had fragmented and needed a retrieval.

There were genograms all over my dining room table. Genograms are family trees that therapists use as a tool to gather family information. I had poster boards with elaborate trees. Every free waking second, I was drawing and connecting cousins to their parents based on the family trees I could find on Ancestry. I called my maternal uncle, who unfortunately had dementia. He remembered me but didn't remember much of anything else. I spoke to his wife, my aunt, who only relayed a story of my mom's older sister, who had an affair in the late 50s, early 60s. Oddly enough, I knew the story already because I remembered my mother told me about it when I was incredibly young. My aunt apparently had a boyfriend whom she loved very much. She already had children and a husband whom everyone adored. My aunt was toying with the idea of leaving her husband for another man. I am not sure how the rest of the family figured it out, but they made my aunt's life a living hell. My aunt stayed with her husband.

My aunt confirmed what my mother had told me, that my aunt was the target of a great deal of flack when she was considering leaving her husband for her paramour. My mother never judged her sister. I remember her telling me the story as a matter of fact. Perhaps my mother was telling me a bit of her story, my story too, but I was too young to make connections or be suspicious of my mom's past. Under those circumstances though, I would bet my mother's impropriety was never shared with anyone in her family, even her sister, who she was close to. My mother would never subject herself to the punishment she witnessed her sister go through for the same adulterous crime. My mom had a con-sequence other than family admonishment. My mom had me. It is a tad strange that a mom would share the story about my aunt with her child. I was probably around eleven or twelve years old when she told me.

My aunt couldn't help me. She just assured me I was loved. It felt like platitudes. "But you look just like him!" That was something I heard from many of my relatives once I shared my findings.

Those genograms led me to a man who was exactly the same age as my mother. He had crystal blue eyes and I am sure I met him at church. He was an usher. I couldn't remember if it was at Sacred Heart or St. Michael's, but I recognized his face. If he was the winner of the "I Fathered Alexandra" prize, it would make sense. He was born the same year as my mother and they both lived in the same town, Lyndhurst, NJ, where I grew up. My mom had an affinity for men with pretty eyes. This guy could very well be the winner. I contacted several people in my alleged family. The first was someone who may have been my brother. He was a cantankerous man.

Mr. Cantankerous was a professional who lived and worked in the next town over from where we had lived in Ocean County. Mr. Cantankerous was abrupt and offered terse answers about how he didn't care about his brothers and that his parents were dead. He made it clear he wanted nothing to do with me at all and seemed angry that I called him. How dare I. Mr. Cantankerous may be no different from the new biological brother I encountered later in my discovery, but at least Mr. Cantankerous was willing to talk with me. He wasn't a total jerk, just an angry man.

To be fair, I left a message on Mr. Cantankerous' phone with no hint what I was calling him for. Mr. Cantankerous probably thought it was a business call, and I was a potential customer. I was completely void of tact while I was looking for "the one." I did not know if father dearest was alive or dead. If this particular blue-eyed beauty was my father, he was most likely deceased, as he would be over a hundred years old. I spoke to another new cousin on my list who had an extensive family tree built. Nancy was so kind and from California. Nancy and I exchanged phone numbers. We had several conversations, and she was very understanding and compassionate and proud to welcome me to the family. Nancy shared that Mr. Cantankerous had an evil reputation within the extended family. I came to find out how large my extended family really was. "We are a lot of loud Italians," Nancy shared. I was lucky enough to talk with Nancy's mom. Her dad had passed away. Nancy's dad was my alleged biological father's cousin. Nancy also had half siblings. Half siblings were two foreign words that have grown too familiar to me. I was zeroing in. Nancy's mom shared that my alleged bio father was a bit of a "run around" who had a girlfriend or two on the side. In fact, I was asked if my mother's name was Angie because apparently, the three boys' mothers used to threaten them when they misbehaved, that she would send them to live with Angie. I spoke with Claire, another cousin who didn't know much about anyone in her distant family. Claire was also very compassionate and kind towards me. Claire's caution was, "Don't rush, you are processing a great deal here. You must be kind to yourself." Claire was right. I felt completely lost. I was void of kindness towards myself. Kindness meant self-care. Self-care was nonexistent.

As I was going through the process of trying to figure out who was my biological father, the fury within me grew and festered like an infected boil. I realized that if my mother was alive, I would have strangled her. The mere thought of her face made me cringe, and I never thought I was capable of the anger I felt inside me. That fierce, oppressive anger burned hot and persisted for several weeks. I was getting closer to the truth, but how dare my mother cheat on my dad? How could she do that to him? He was such a wonderful man. He was Santa Claus at Christmas. My dad was kind, generous, talented, and funny. Everyone loved my dad. Amid the sadness, along with being completely overwhelmed, functioning on little to no sleep and a great deal of crying, the intensity of overwhelming emotions was often too much to bear. My blood pressure rose and over the next few months, the stress of this discovery and not knowing who my biological father was took its toll on me physically. I developed shingles because of what was happening to me mentally and emotionally. I couldn't reconcile how my mother could do this to my dad. The paradox, I also realized, was that if my mother didn't cheat on my dad, I wouldn't be here. We all make ourselves the subject and others become objects, clearly a simplistic and reactive process.

I continued to search, pull up pictures, and talk to distant relatives. I thought that once I was completely sure, I would know on some deep cosmic level and I was not feeling it with the blue-eyed usher from the church. Eventually, the person I thought was the lucky winner of who fathered Alexandra was not who I thought. I received a phone call from Anastasia almost two weeks after my discovery. "Call Agnes," she said. "She knows something." I hadn't talked to Agnes in ten years. I received obligatory sisterly birthday cards from her every year which only upset me because it felt hypocritical to me. "She said to look up the name Barrie," said Anastasia. I told her I didn't think it was Barrie. I had narrowed it down to another name. I went to sleep that night and woke up at 1:00am in a start. I remembered seeing the Barrie name in someone else's genogram. I was getting used to early morning jolts of subconscious information surfacing into my awareness. Booting up the computer, something I was now accustomed to at oddball hours, became a regular occurrence. I found the last name Barrie as she had said. It was appended to Cousin Luigi's family tree and I didn't know how I had missed it.

The next day I called Agnes. I thought I had closed that chapter in the book. I knew I might try to reconnect. This was one of the most vulnerable moments of my life. I didn't want to talk to Agnes, but I was desperate. I needed to know the truth. I wanted the nightmare to be over and I mistakenly thought the truth would do that. Agnes told me the story of Frank Barrie. He was a friend of "mommy and daddy's." Frank was around the house all the time back in the day. Frank would spend time with mommy and have cocktails with her when daddy was out bowling. Frank Barrie was a handsome, nice young man with political aspirations, not much older than Agnes. After a while apparently, my dad, for some reason, told Frank Barrie not to come back to the house. Frank was officially banned forever. I would have banned him too if he was messing around with my wife. Agnes said Frank was "really nice." Agnes also wasn't sure if Frank Barrie would still be alive because someone in the family had died tragically in a car crash. Agnes said mom was reading the *Herald News* and was crying and screaming hysterically and my dad said under his breath and uncharacteristically mean for him, "Too bad it was the wrong brother."

Agnes told me she and Anastasia found a picture of Frank Barrie in my mother's belongings when Anastasia was visiting her home two years ago. Agnes questioned Anastasia and said, "Who do you think Frank looks like?" Anastasia shrugged her shoulders. "Doesn't Frank look like Alexandra? I think this is Alexandra's biological father." Anastasia urged her to throw the picture away. Anastasia had a famous saying, "When in doubt, throw it out." Sure, throw it out, forget about it, sweep it under the rug. If we don't acknowledge this fact, then it did not happen. It's amazing to me that my right to know was never a thought in either of their heads. Let's stay in denial. This is where I differ from my originals. I prefer facing life head-on, whether or not I want to. This was a choice I made throughout my life. Ignoring something or pretending it wasn't there didn't work for me (like Anastasia ignoring me on the floor with her boyfriend wrapped around my legs). It left me in disarray. Agnes kept the picture, telling me that I was already not talking to her and she didn't want to make matters worse by telling me that my dad might not have been my biological father.

Agnes told me she felt better telling me this now, so that she didn't have to take this secret to her grave. The lost Catholic in me wanted to offer penance and absolution. Seriously, how gallant. I hope this eased her guilty little conscience. I felt like I was lied to yet another time. What an awful feeling that was. So much for any hope of reconciliation here. There are no hopes for reconciliation when trust is nonexistent. I had already been struggling with trust issues and questioning the motives of my parents. My intellectual side understood the reasons for protection. The emotional side of me felt betrayed and lied to. Who were they protecting? My parents did not owe me anything except the truth. If there was doubt with the two people I trusted most in my life, I was sure I did not have the where-with-all to work on trust with my originals anymore, not without family therapy, which would never happen in this lifetime.

Anastasia took part in this original discussion with Agnes, made me call Agnes, and failed to tell me anything while I was begging her to take a DNA test because someone made a mistake. Agnes confirmed a secret she kept, which directly affected me and my right to know. Agnes and Anastasia's dirty little secret was out. They talked about my paternity probabilities years earlier before I knew anything. I was bound and determined to not be anyone's dirty little secret anymore. I stayed in touch for a brief time after that, but Agnes stopped answering because my text messages included more than she asked for and because she was "too deeply affected" by my DNA discovery. Her usual, "How do you think I feel?" prevailed. Forgiveness does not mean you have to resume a relationship. Writing about it brings up the feelings and I remind myself that, like the good book says, forgiveness is seventy times seven. I must keep on forgiving until the pain is gone. Pain, they say, helps you to grow. I may never get over this DNA discovery, but I am bound and determined to get through it.

Agnes texted me the picture of my biological father. I always thought that when I saw a picture, I would just know and recognize my father in my gut. I was right. The picture came across my phone. Agnes kept the original. She never sent it to me as she promised. Agnes held it hostage. But I knew the second I laid eyes on Frank Barrie that he was the lucky winner. I had goose-bumps and chills the second I laid eyes on him. What was amazing was that even though the picture was in black and white, I was looking into eyes that looked like they belonged to me. I found him within two weeks. I found my biological father. Then I fell apart again.

The roller coaster ride had so many trials and tribulations which continue, even today. One moment I was fine. The next moment I was crying my eyes out. Unless you live the experience, you may not understand and that is okay with me. I am not looking for total understanding, just acceptance, honesty, and respect. I would like to have my whole situation fixed. The fact is, there is no fixing to be done, only reality to contend with.

Out came the genograms again, along with the name Frank Barrie. I was piecing together his family, my new family. I found plenty of information via Ancestry. I had three aunts, an uncle, and much to my surprise, I had a little brother and a little sister. Discovering that I had two younger siblings was the first moment that brought me joy. We grew up one town away from each other, a ten-minute car ride. I rode my bicycle across the Kingsland Avenue Bridge many times to their town. Once I deciphered birthday and death dates, I still wasn't sure if Frank Barrie was alive or not. Soon into these findings, I uncovered something incredibly major that I never would have expected.

I always thought my mother was a woman ahead of her time. But there were some parts of the puzzle that I had never considered. My father, Frank Barrie, was twenty years younger than my mother. My mother was a cougar.

3

THE ADVENTURE BEGINS

"A Half-truth is a white lie."
—Yiddish Proverb

Frank Barrie worked with my mom in a travel/insurance and real estate agency. My mother was a travel agent. I knew the winner of who fathered Alexandra was someone my mother worked with because throughout my life, she always seemed to work. It made sense that I came to be because of an office love affair. I met no one from this agency, and because I was a dead ringer for the old man, I understood why.

I called my niece Gwen, Agnes' daughter, who's five years younger than me. I told her what happened. I told her my mother was a cougar. Gwen giggled and said, "Go nana, go nana!" in a sing-songy voice. I didn't laugh and after we hung up, I cried. She called back the next day and apologized. Forgiveness was granted. Forgiveness has become the F word, not a favorite, but compulsory sometimes for my survival. I wasn't ready for levity yet, although I have a sense of humor which has always gotten me through the worst of times.

The Barrie family genogram was spread across my table. I had to figure out how to proceed. I searched social media and found my brother Moshe with his family. He was wearing a yarmulke. Reality hit home at a speed I wasn't ready for. Everything I found made me cry. I couldn't locate my sister on social media, but I knew she was out there. These new siblings were younger than me. I was beyond excited to learn I had young nephews I could spoil and get to know and love because I love kids, especially when they are my kin.

I watched a few videos of my brother marketing his law practice. He seemed so approachable and friendly. I got up my nerve and, with a shaky voice, I called Moshe's office. A very protective assistant with a thick North Jersey regional accent informed me that Mr. Barrie would be available after one in the afternoon that day. Pins and needles followed for the next four hours. I called back at one fifteen. I felt like I was going to throw up. The same assistant told me that the best way to reach Mr. Barrie was via email, since he hadn't returned to the office yet. So, I gave it my best college try while trying not to sound as unhinged as I was:

Alexandra A Barrie <alexandraabarrie@gmail.com>

Mon, Apr 16, 2018

Hi Moshe,

I hope you are well. Your assistant gave me your email address. I am looking to locate Frank Barrie.

*Is he related to you? I believe he was involved in insurance (Barrie and Smith) as was my mother (the Farmer Agency in *****, NJ). Frank knew my mother before he was married. She has been gone since 2004 and my pop died in 2002. I did an ancestry test and learned that I was Eastern European, Jewish, and Sicilian to name the top three. My mother was Polish but the dad I loved with all my heart was Swedish and Canadian French. Neither of those were present in the results.*

My sister has my parents' belongings up in Maine. I am in Florida. Among the pictures, she found a large picture of Mr. Barrie and a smaller article dated 5/3/62 from the Passaic Herald News (we are all from Lyndhurst). From what she tells me, Mr. Barrie spent a great deal of time at our home. She said something about a bad car accident and told me my mother was real upset. Apparently, though this sounds a bit muddled, and I don't mean it to be—it was how it was reported to me—my father stopped allowing him to come to our home. I was born in 1961.

I am a professional, my kids are all grown, I live in Florida now but still come back to NJ to visit—I am just looking for answers. If Mr. Barrie is who I think he may be, I would love to talk with him. I am hoping he could shed some light on everything for me.

I am working at home today—my private cell phone is xxx-xxx-xxxx. I am reachable until 5pm and then I am working for two hours and free after 7pm.

Thank you for your kindness,

Alexandra A. Barrie

I waited for that phone call for what felt like an eternity. I stayed glued to my phone with a knot in my chest the size of a beach ball. The next day, after receiving no response at all, I sent another email:

Alexandra A Barrie <alexandraabarrie@gmail.com>

Tue, Apr 17, 2018

Hi again,

I meant to send you these yesterday. It's a text that my sister sent me from Maine and also a picture of me. I also didn't tell you that my mother's name is Irene Pedersen and my father is

*Lou Pedersen, Sr. We lived on Lively Terrace in ********.*

Two years ago, my sister found a large picture and I guess this newspaper clipping as well. I didn't know anything about it then. One sister told the other sister to throw it out. My guess is my mother was following Frank Barrie's progress in politics.

In any event, I sent you this because I want to be transparent here. I am working on an updated Genogram which I'd be happy to share because I have so much information it's a bit overwhelming. I wish I could've spoken to you by phone instead of via email. I just hope you're getting my emails.

I wasn't terribly interested in staying on ancestry.com – until this snafu. I really felt that I would be going to visit the French-Canadian cousins this summer LOL. At this point, I'm not even sure who knows and who doesn't know.

*I'm a therapist, by the way. I had an office in ****** New Jersey for five years (and a few other locations) and closed it in June. I had an office in New Jersey and Florida but closed one because the traveling was too much. So now I consult at a hospital. I specialize in developmental disorders. I also have a private practice. I understand if you're not ready to answer me—please just let me know you received this.*

Thanks, Alexandra

I included the picture Agnes sent me of our father and a picture of me so he could see some of the family resemblance. Moshe never answered me. I was completely ignored and have not been acknowledged to this day. I do not know why. People ask me why Moshe won't speak with me, like I have all the answers. I get showered with reasons, usually cutting Moshe a break. Maybe Moshe was traumatized too. After all, in its infancy stage, this DNA discovery raised so many questions about our parents. Moshe, as an attorney, most likely thought I wanted money. That's probably at least one component of the reason. Not knowing his relationship with his mother and our father, it would be safe to hypothesize there are other reasons, but they would only be conjecture. Frankly, no pun intended, I don't care. It is clearly not about me (in spite of the fact that I am the center of the universe). Remembering how we all felt about Jeannie's new sister, I thought I would go to Moshe first as logically, he might be concerned that I was looking for the Barrie family fortune. It made sense before I reached out to Frank Barrie to approach Moshe so that the transparency would be obvious. I found a death record with Frank Barrie's name but no birth record, so I wasn't sure if it was the same person or not. I found so many of the "old country relatives," married cousins with the same last name. Besides, if he was alive, I didn't want to cause a cardiac event.

Was my biological father alive? I was looking for confirmation of him being alive or dead. The online services had his age right, but I couldn't find an obituary. I was still new to researching on the Ancestry site. I must admit, the thought of finding another father, at my age, was rather exciting. There was enough love in my heart to love a father I never knew. At least I believed that. I still do. I lost my dad, Lou, just after I turned forty-one. I missed having parents to love and talk with. I allowed myself to engage in magical thinking that the long-lost daughter would appear and bring happiness to all. The truth was, my presence caused some confusion for my elderly aunts at first, some disbelief and then happiness for my sister, and obvious ambivalence for Moshe. If I had another father out there, a biological one who was still alive, I wanted to look him directly in the eyes and hear his side of the story, my story, our story.

I did not sleep over four hours a night for several weeks. Why wasn't this lawyer brother of mine calling me back? Does he have any empathy? I didn't get it. I thought he might be a family man. His YouTube videos made him appear very genuine and approachable. Moshe might be someone I could like. He should know all the referrals I could have sent him. My son needed a lawyer, and I told him to call the Barrie Law Firm and tell them, "Your sister sent me." He even played "the family card" as the reason he pursued law in one of those "I am a human lawyer" videos. He told cyberspace land he became an attorney because a family member had an accident and the mom could not afford to take legal action against the perpetrator. The least he could do was acknowledge me, tell me to go to hell if that made him happy.

I gave up on receiving a phone call from brother dearest after the first three years. Sometimes I will send a message of cheer around the holidays but, like Linda, those messages were never acknowledged. I wanted to call my new sister, but I felt the need to protect her. So, I went to the youngest of my father's siblings on the list, Lori. Ironically, Lori lived the next town over from me when we lived in NJ prior to moving to Florida. Through research, I found out that she was a therapist too. Our vocation got me thinking about nurture v. nature. Is being a therapist genetic? People used to tell me there was another clinician in the next town who could be my sister. I would always laugh and tell them that everyone had an evil twin. I heard a shaky voice on the other end of the phone once I explained who I was. I told Lori I knew I had a brother and sister. I asked for verification of Frank Barrie's birthdate and if he died in April 1993. She said, "I have to call Moshe and ask him if it is okay." I told her I tried to reach Moshe, but he wasn't answering me. Lori wasn't budging and would not tell me anything. She told me Moshe was a "really nice guy." Everyone is entitled to their opinion. My sixth sense told me I just hit another roadblock. I wrote Lori a letter with facts I had uncovered and a copy of our family's genogram and some pictures with hopes that there might be a family resemblance she would connect to. I hoped maybe because we were in the same field, Lori would be more understanding. I sent the letter via snail mail.

I was still tired, sad, frustrated, and even more pissed off at my mother. Sleep evaded me on yet another night. The next morning, bound and determined and ready to transcend all roadblocks, I called the Jewish cemetery listed on the death notice of Frank Barrie, and a busy Jersey accent answered my call and confirmed my father's death, age of death, and next of kin. That was one mystery solved. Now came the project of putting together exactly who Frank Barrie was and where did I come from? What was this new culture I inherited and knew next to nothing about? Was my whole life a lie?

I grieved for a full day that this new father of mine was dead. He was dead! I thought I was silly for being so sad and feeling the loss I was suffering. The loss felt undeniably palpable. I thought I was being ridiculous. I invalidated my own feelings. How can you possibly feel sadness for someone you have never met? Trust me, you can. It is even feasible that once you find out more about that person through those left behind, that love is a possibility.

Being "ghosted" as we call it in NPE land, is common with many people who discover they have new families. Ghosting is not responding and is exactly what Moshe elected to do. Being ignored felt humiliating and demoralizing. Feeling invisible had to be contended with but it is not easy. After all, I promised myself I would be nobody's dirty little secret. Sometimes, my NPE associates reported that there were threats made to take legal action. Sometimes, there were comments angrily wishing someone well after they just found out this news, this horrible, earth-shattering news. It can get nasty. I never received that cease-and-desist order from my brother, the lawyer. I waited but thank God it never came. I dreamed of leaving nasty reviews on google exposing Moshe, but the truth is, I knew on some level he was also suffering through this and that maybe we were more alike than we were different. After all, we share the same genes and the same slightly crooked smile. I hated the fact that I was feeling compassionate towards the little brother who ignored me. What is wrong with me?

Because of the state I was in, my niece Gwen implored me to

take another DNA test with another company, just to be sure. I ordered a 23andMe DNA test next to placate her. Gwen was convinced this DNA business was all a mistake. I thought I might find some more answers. I gave up on reaching out to anyone but promised myself that once my 23andMe results were in, I would continue my mission to connect to the family I never knew I had. Ironically enough, I was satisfied with my decision to completely disconnect from my original siblings. I was okay. Why would I want to discover a whole new set of issues with a whole new group of people? Chances are, since I am older and my new family is older, I would find myself in with a family of people who would trigger my official "issue beeper" (my personal phrase). So, what changed? I don't know. Brand-new issues? My intuition guided my path. I already knew I would not meet my biological father. My work taught me that as far as families go, there are levels of functionality. I never believed in dysfunctional families. The perfect ones, I contended, were just better about hiding their family secrets. Every family has an Agnes, and every family has a Moshe. With my originals, our shared experiences seemed to be what kept us attached. Now that I have been around a family block a few times, I know that there is no such thing as a utopian family and I knew enough to ward off all hopes of a ghost kingdom as the adoptees call it. (A ghost kingdom is a fantasy where an adoptee imagines the perfect biological family.)

Another round of spit was mailed off to 23andMe along with registration, etc. I was in my office when I received notification that my results were in. This time I also ordered a health report so that I could look at my health history genetics. Since my dad was not my biological father, I had unwittingly given false information to many doctors and insurance carriers. I was most concerned now about Tay Sachs, at this point. I worried my own kids could be carriers for this disease, which mostly affects Jewish people. There is also an increase in the likelihood of breast cancer for Ashkenazi Jews. Fortunately, I am not a carrier for Tay Sachs, and

I don't have the breast cancer variant. I let my brother Moshe, know via email, even though he still wasn't talking to me.

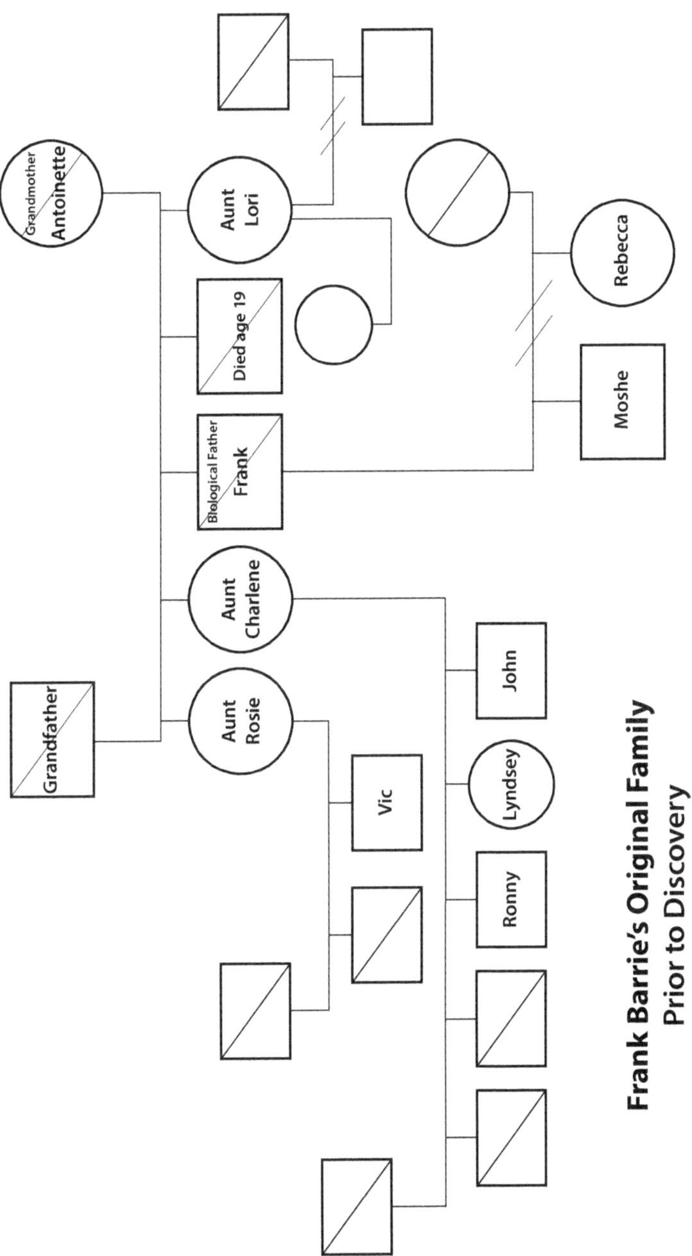

Frank Barrie's Original Family
Prior to Discovery

I was on a break for lunch, and I opened my 23AndMe report. My Aunt Charlene, the second oldest in my father's family, was right there, listed as my aunt on the report. I wrote her an email and called her and left a message. It was Saturday morning. I found my new sister Rebecca's landline number, and left a message. I did not mention Frank Barrie. She never called me back. When I told my niece Gwen, she laughed and said, "She probably thought you were a telemarketer." I found out later on that Rebecca had received my message. Rebecca's boss and I shared the same name, though she did not recognize the voice. Ergo, since I have pleasant phone etiquette, Rebecca thought that yes, I was a telemarketer and did not call me back.

Aunt Charlene called me back. She went online and saw the results of the DNA test but did not make the aunt/niece connection. She explained that her mother was adopted and that she had hoped to find out some information about her heritage and possible family. Charlene said she knew of my mother and that her brother Frank said he had caught my mother fooling around with the owner of the agency. I knew enough about how my mother spoke about the owner that it could not have happened the way Frank told Charlene. I refused to believe my mother was a Jezebel and double standards are not permitted in my brain. Having too many lovers would have posed too much of a mind screw for my mom. I knew that at the core of my being. I was conflicted. Of course, the thought crossed my mind that my mother might be some kind of slutty woman since I was already angry with her. I knew in my gut it really wasn't so. Charlene said that the owner of the agency was most likely my father. I knew he was not related by blood to this family and he did not show up in any of my DNA connections. Aunt Charlene showed up as my aunt. I didn't argue. I had to give up so I wouldn't cause a problem for Charlene. She was older, and she spent a lot of time on the phone talking to me. Aunt Charlene was kind and compassionate.

The next day I was leaving for New Jersey. I had hoped to have some genuine answers by then and maybe meet with a member of my new family. I was attending a colleague's master's degree ceremony. My husband dropped me off at the airport around seven in the morning. At seven forty, I opened the email I saw yesterday as I was waiting for the airport tram. I was hoping to hear more information from my new family. Following is our exchange:

Charlene Loventhall to me:

Mon, May 14, 2018

it looks like i am your aunt my daughter helped me figure it out

Alexandra Barrie to Charlene:

May 14, 2018

Then I consider myself lucky. You are very kind.

Hugs,

Alexandra

Charlene Loventhall to me:

May 15, 2018

let's keep in touch. let me know when you will be in jersey

I headed towards airport security when my phone rang with a local NJ phone number. I quickly answered. "Hello, this is Rebecca Barrie. I am Frank Barrie's daughter." "Well then," I answered, with a smile in my voice and on my face as big as the Cheshire cat, "I guess that makes you my little sister." I was smiling in my heart. Then, the unthinkable happened. I told Rebecca I had just entered security and would have to hang up and call her back. I just could not believe it. I waited all this time to talk with Rebecca and I had to hang up on her. My insides were doing cartwheels. What if I called back and she didn't answer? What if having to hang up upsets her? Now what do I do, step off to the side? I don't want to miss my flight to New Jersey.

Once I got through security, there was an email waiting for me because Rebecca had to leave for work. Apparently, Moshe called Rebecca and let her know that they had an "alleged sister." Moshe forwarded the email that I sent him to Rebecca. Rebecca confirmed my information in the email and told me that the person who died in the car accident that upset my mother years ago, was not my father but his younger brother. This happened in Monmouth County, about a mile from where my office was located forty years later. Rebecca said the whole family never recovered. We agreed to speak again later in the afternoon, after my plane landed. Rebecca gave me her work schedule so we could talk. Rebecca called me on her lunch break as I was driving through Toms River. Her high-speed New Jersey accent was filled with more information about our family and she agreed to meet with me during this trip. My thoughts were whirling through my head at the speed of Rebecca's rapid speech. We were both emotionally charged. I went to the graduation the next day, and the following day I made plans to drive to my hometown over an hour away and meet my sister for the first time in our lives. She was turning fifty in a few weeks, and I was fifty-seven. This experience was beyond surreal. I was exhausted and excited, and I would have a plane to catch at six in the morning from an airport over two hours away from my hotel.

Rebecca met me at one of my favorite diners. If you know New Jersey, you know they have the best diners. I spent the afternoon with my youngest son who lives in NJ. We ate pizza, and I met his latest girlfriend, and I had an acute case of agita. I just wanted to go north, and I was not entirely present that afternoon. During the late afternoon, I started on my schlep up north. Fortunately, I drove against the traffic on the Garden State Parkway until I got closer to Newark. I felt like crying. I was choked up, but the tears wouldn't come. Besides, I didn't want to look like a mess the first time I met my sister. My agita never improved. Rebecca was standing, holding the door of the Lyndhurst Diner, smiling. I still wanted to cry. We gave each other a great big hug. I knew everything would be okay. The two of us were ushered to our table complete with Lyndhurst diner placemats and a menu which contained my favorite cheeseburger, Diet Coke, and cheesecake for dessert. After looking into each other's eyes, we ordered our food and Rebecca exchanged a few text messages back and forth from her husband and Moshe, reassuring them I was not an ax murderer. The two of us talked like we knew each other our whole lives. One of the best parts about having my world completely turned topsy-turvy was, and is, my sister Rebecca. She has been the light in all of this. I love my cousins and aunts too, but my little sister is delightful.

Rebecca asked a server to take some pictures for us. Feeling a little paranoid, I had hoped the server would not recognize me, fearing my parents' secret would be out in the open. This was still a fresh wound opened again and again and I was in the completely unchartered waters of my conflicted emotions. I consciously masked my internal world with a smile. Being in home territory was strangely not comforting. I still didn't know how to handle all of this. It felt like I was cutting school and stupidly going to the local diner where the fear sets in that the principal might show up for lunch at any minute. Rebecca proudly explained to the server we were sisters who just met. She was quick to grab my hands and make me feel like everything would be okay. Rebecca was beaming. Amidst the trauma, she was indeed a ray of hope for me.

I drove back from the diner to the Jersey Shore and talked with Jay, my husband, on the Bluetooth phone in the car all the way back to my hotel. Jay had been, and continues to be, such a grounding force in my life with all of this. I would not have survived without him. I knew I had an early morning flight to catch, so when I got back to the hotel, I packed my bag for my return to

Florida. Somehow, this trip was a whirlwind. I did not sleep one ounce that night. I signed on to social media after midnight and I talked with my cousin from California who knew I had found my family, and though I tried to sleep, sleep continued to evade me. I had to leave in a few hours to be at the airport at an ungodly hour of the morning. Jay would meet me at Tampa International in a few hours, and I needed a hug. I returned home to an email with pictures of my biological father. Rebecca sent them. "That first one looks just like you."

There was more to follow as that first year, prior to the pandemic, I did a lot of traveling up north to connect to these people who were virtual strangers. Love. Somewhere in all of this, we found love and connection.

4

Divine Debutante Debut

*"You have to leave the city of your comfort and go into the wilderness of your own intuition. What you'll discover will be wonderful.
What you'll discover is yourself."*
—Alan Alda

The first several months of my NPE experience were surreal. Though it was painful in the beginning, over a period, if you are open to it, you learn you grow through pain. If I could say one thing about my growing pains, well, at least they were consistent. I had boarded the emotional roller coaster ride each week until the consistency changed to biweekly and then sporadically. Occasionally, the roller coaster would hit a bump and nearly derail. But I am still here. I had days where I felt like a socially incompetent ninny telling everyone who made eye contact with me my story, days where my negative self-talk got the best of me, and days where I was completely elated that I had a second chance with my newfound family.

After speaking with Aunt Charlene several times, I decided it was now time to call Aunt number three, the eldest and the matriarch of sorts, Aunt Rosie, who answered the phone on my first attempt.

"Hello, this is Alexandra Pedersen calling. Is this Miss Rose?" I did not know what to call this woman and figured I would wait until my aunts instructed me what they wanted me to call them. So far, I only had one of three consistently talking to me.

"Oh! It's you! You have been causing quite the stir in this family!" she bellowed.

I kept thinking that I should be scared, terrified, petrified enough to maybe hang up or something. I fought back the urge to blubber like the mealy-mouthed pathetic loser my inner critic encouraged me to be. "I know, I know, I'm sorry," I wanted to cower. Instead, I stood strong. I do not know where the strength in me came from. "I beg to differ with you, ma'am. I am not the one who caused the stir." Wow, I was brave. Was that me that just said that? It's a damn good thing Aunt Rosie couldn't see my face.

I explained my mis-attributed parentage. I told her Aunt Charlene gave me her phone number. She asked about my mother. I was still angry at my mother. I told her my mother and Frank worked together and that my mother was twenty years older than my father.

"What are your goals in all of this?"

Shit! Goals? I have no freakin' idea what my goals are. Am I supposed to have goals? My instinct was running the show. My intellect and sense of reasoning were out the window. "I am not sure." I became instantly defensive. I was sad. I wished I hadn't met any of these people. I wished I never took a DNA test for fun to go visit relatives in Sweden and Canada that I could no longer claim as my own.

"So, your mother was Mrs. Robinson," Aunt Rosie was clearly annoyed with my mother, Irene. That was the end of me. I thought I was going to die right there and then. Somebody else said what I had been singing since the beginning.

"That's what I was calling her too," I said sadly. There's nothing like getting the wrecking ball out now, go ahead, Aunt Rosie. She was in for the kill, and I didn't know it until the jackhammer hit me in the head. "My brother died, and I would prefer that he rest in peace. Good luck to you and whatever your desires are as far as all of this goes. I really have no interest in this. My brother deserves to rest in peace."

How dare she call my mother Mrs. Robinson! Only I can call her that. I was heartbroken and held on to my hysteria in silence until I hung up the phone. I skated into the next room where Jay was working.

"You will not believe what happened," sobbing as usual. I did a lot of crying back then. To think that there were any tears left in me was unimaginable. I told Jay the story in between tears. There was no sleeping for me that night either. I was beside myself. How disconcerting! How unconscionable! Who talks to people like that?

"You know," said Jay, "she sounds pretty direct." Direct? She was blunt.

"You and your aunt seem to have a lot in common," he said. So now he is telling me I am straightforward and unconscionable? I always said I appreciated straight-talking individuals, honest folks who do not do the Watutsi around the truth as I was accustomed to. Jay was right. I was thinking to myself that she would be sorry because I was a genuine human being. I don't do phony very well. It would take me a while to recover from THAT phone call.

Well, I called Aunt Charlene to let her know I reached out to Aunt Rosie.

"Oh, you did?" her voice was smiling. "How did that go?"

"Not very well," I replied. "She wished me well and told me she was going to let her brother rest in peace."

Later on, my sister and cousin both asked me why I didn't let them know I was calling Aunt Rosie. Rebecca asked, "Why didn't you tell me you were calling her? When she gets angry, she punches couches and curses people out. She's a lot like Frank." My sweet cousin Lyndsey replied, "You should have told me. I would have warned you." So, if I am a lot like Aunt Rosie and Aunt Rosie is a lot like my biological father, then my social skills needed some attention.

There were many more phone calls. Aunt Charlene and I spoke on the phone. Rebecca and I texted and talked regularly. It's strange and wonderful that I was accepted so easily into this part of my new family. Jay flew up for a visit with me, too. It was important to me that he meet my new family since he had to deal with my traumatic responses daily. He nursed my shingles, which came on three months after my discovery, held me when I cried, and sat for hours with me trying to make suppositions on the Frank and Irene story. He even helped me vilify Moshe.

Jay, Rebecca, and I headed for Aunt Charlene's home in northern Bergen County. We drove the same route my mother and I drove together when I worked with her in the summers in my teenage years. My paternal grandmother frequented the shop across the street from our office. I was sure I must have passed her a dozen times or more during several years of employment with my mom. On some level, it almost felt like my ancestors were riding in the car with us sitting in the back seat with me. I felt enveloped and overwhelmed at the same time. Jay and Rebecca hit it off. I let her sit in the front seat and she did some backseat driving.

"See?" I said to Jay. "It runs in the family."

"It isn't anything that a little duct tape couldn't fix," said Jay.

We laughed and Jay and Rebecca had some minor, fun-loving bickering going on. In New Jersey, if you are not being teased or made fun of by loved ones, there is something wrong with you.

Before leaving to meet Aunt Charlene, Rebecca and I went to the local grocery shop where my dad and mom shopped every week. It felt a little odd. I was in my hometown at my dad's favorite grocery store, buying flowers for a new family. I decided on daisies (inspired by my mother, who loved daisies), and I had the woman behind the counter wrap the daisies with a lavender bow. My intuition and my mother's spirit guided me well. Aunt Charlene's favorite flower was daisies, and she told me that purple is her favorite color. I wanted for Aunt Charlene to like me. I wanted my new family to accept me. I wanted to connect, and it was happening without me being cognizant of the slow and steady transformation from stranger to new sister, new niece, and new cousin.

Aunt Charlene greeted us at the front door of her lovely home in Bergen County, NJ. It was the home where she raised five children. It was a little awkward being studied by my cousin and my aunt. My irrational thoughts kicked in as though I was some kind of imposter who was fabricating this nightmare for attention. I was feeling naked and exposed again. My cousin Lyndsey examined every move I made and finally reported,

"Even her mannerisms are like Aunt Lori's."

Rebecca had sent me pictures of Aunt Lori and reported that we both looked like her. There was a picture of Aunt Lori with blonde hair about ten years ago that I looked at and was floored. It was amazing to be with people whom I resembled. Many NPEs who meet family for the first time share this feeling. I was always the dark-haired, tall kid in the family picture filled with blondes and a redhead. When I meet a fellow NPE, one of our first discussions was how it felt to not look like anyone in the family. Of course, there are a few who are lucky enough to look like their mother, so at least they look like somebody, but the rest of us all seem to favor our biological father's looks. While I was growing up, there were always some cheesy jokes made about me being the daughter of the laundryman. I made light of it too, without being cognizant of the truth that stared me straight in the face. "My mother was a travel agent? What else would you expect?" and everyone laughed. I resembled my new family, including Rebecca and Aunt Lori.

My first visit to Aunt Charlene's was a fabulous, incredible homecoming. Once we moved past my resemblance to Aunt Lori, with ooos and aaaahs from my cousin, Jay and I were ushered into Aunt Charlene's dining room. Aunt Charlene prepared a homecoming feast that was esthetically pleasing and delectably delicious. It felt as though I was starring in a movie about the long-lost child who came home to her family, a family she had never known. The home had aromas of freshly baked bread and Italian food. I felt wanted. I felt like I belonged. I felt like I was finally home.

Aunt Charlene outdid herself. There were sausage and peppers, bagels with an array of cream cheeses, lox, capers, and rugalach, hallah bread, cakes, all homemade. Aunt Charlene is a well-known baker in her circles, and her circles comprised friends, business associates, and acquaintances. Aunt Charlene exuded a warm, welcoming spirit. She was the first official Barrie to accept me into the family. "We have had so many losses in this family," Aunt Charlene shared, "Finding out my brother Frank had a daughter, and you are part of our family now can only be positive. This is not a loss; it is a gain." Aunt Charlene had a very close relationship with my biological father and would speak of him often. I loved to hear stories about my bio father as it helped me to form a relationship with this man I never knew. I was getting to know him now.

Aunt Charlene introduced me to Ronny and John, two of my new first cousins. John lived with her, and Ronny had a family of his own. Ronny proudly showed me pictures of his children. Ronny said he told Moshe he was going to meet me. We all giggled because Moshe made a quick escape because I was in town. I was thinking he left for Canada. We plotted that we should all go find him. We did a lot of laughing that day.

Jay and I ate and talked with my new family. They welcomed

both of us. I will hold on to that memory until my last breath. Aunt Charlene made coffee, and the cousins sat around the table. My cousins clued me in on family stories about a variety of issues. There was no sarcasm, no judgment, something I had grown accustomed to and avoided in my original family. For being so new to all of this, I was welcomed into a very intimate world where I belonged. I was home.

Aunt Charlene told me stories about life with Frank and the fun they had together. She preserved my biological father's memory while reminiscing about pleasant joyful moments of growing up and sticking together. She seemed to forget and forgive any negative attributes he may have had. She giggled as she told me about a party they attended once where my father was drinking too much (from what I heard later, this was not unusual). Frank was asked to leave. Aunt Charlene was right on his tail because, "If he goes, I go." With Frank in the lead, the two of them promptly walked into a closet. She told me that story more than once and delighted in it every time. I seemed to get a snapshot of my father Frank's life from each member of the family. Each new family member I encountered shared something different with me about my biological father.

Jay and I spent four nights in north Jersey on that trip. Most of our activities seemed to center on lavish Italian dinners. The day after our gathering at Aunt Charlene's, Rebecca, Jay, and I had planned to eat at Rutt's Hut. On the way there, I spotted the cemetery where my maternal grandparents were buried. I had not been there in thirty years. Somehow, it felt right to me to pay them a visit. Rebecca found their gravestones. We talked a little about my grandparents and it felt important to me to share some of my past with Rebecca too. My grandparents would have welcomed her with open arms.

That evening, Rebecca and Jason, my new brother-in-law, had a party planned in our honor. Rebecca had told all of her friends that she had a new sister. She wanted everyone close to her to meet me.

I met Rebecca's best friends at my debutante party. Several told me that Rebecca always said that she wanted a sister. Rebecca told me that too. Then something very touching happened. Jason called everyone's attention and there was a toast in my honor. I could see Rebecca tearing up and once again, I found myself speechless. That seemed to happen a lot in the beginning.

Everyone raised their cups in the air and Jason began in a thick North Jersey accent, "So, anyway…. for many years Rebecca would say she wanted a sister."

He continued, "So now she has her sister, and we know God works in strange ways."

"Yes, He does," echoes one of Rebecca's friends.

"Yes, He does," I thought to myself and raised my glass to toast to us.

Jay and I flew back to Florida and if we weren't on a plane, I probably could've flown there myself. I knew I was rising from the ashes. It was the beginning of my healing. It didn't hurt, it felt wonderful. Rebecca and I have a strong family resemblance. She tells me all the time I have the Barrie genes, especially if I say something absurd and we laugh. When she calls, she asks,

"Is this my favorite sister?"

I reply, "I am your only sister, for now."

5

THE NEED FOR GROUNDING

*"Flying starts from the ground. The more grounded you are,
the higher you fly."*
—J.R. Rim

*"So, what is new with you these days, Alexandra?" Giovanni
asked. Gio and Alexandra had been casual friends for several years. Alexandra is in her twentieth year as a therapist.
Giovani is an entrepreneur who has the compassion and the
credentials of being a therapist. Alexandra was telling anyone
her story who would listen at that point, the UPS driver, the
postal worker, the neighborhood dog walker… It was uncharacteristic for Alexandra because she was a professional listener.*

"Well, a lot is new. I am Italian like you now," she answered.

*Giovanni was a bit puzzled. He always thought Alexandra
looked Italian, but she swore she was Swedish and French.
He was clueless about what the hell she was talking about.*

*Alexandra eyed him carefully. She couldn't decide if she
should continue to tell him what was new or not. The truth
was reserved for strangers who wouldn't judge her. Suddenly,
she was feeling like she was on Maury Povich and unwilfully*

naked. She continued, "I did a DNA test, Gio. My dad is not my biological father. Don't mess with me. I am Sicilian! AND Jewish!"

Giovanni was shocked. He had always thought of Alexandra as someone who had her act together. He respected her work, and he appreciated her sense of integrity. This information was delivered out of left field. Giovanni was expecting the rather mundane answer to his question.

Instinctively, he seemed to empathize with what Alexandra was feeling.

"Wow, you know that is traumatic, don't you?" he asked.

"Oh, I am fine," Alexandra responded quickly. She wanted to be normal.

She would do anything to be normal. She was pretending to be normal. Alexandra was feeling as abnormal as you could get.

So began the quest to feel normal again. I ordered DNA tests for everyone during the first year of my discovery. If I was lacking the connection I was yearning for, someone else might have well had it! The first one I begged to get tested was my sister, Anastasia. I needed to see her name appear on the DNA list near mine. In my estimation, Anastasia was scared. She was afraid she might catch what I had, this disease, the cooties, whatever you want to call it. The females in my originals all adored our dad.

I gave a DNA test to my son, to my husband, Jay, to his daughter, and I gave out several DNA kits for Christmas. I desperately needed to be connected to someone through DNA. I needed to see other people I knew be connected to someone they loved. Even if they were not related to me, seeing results connecting those I loved and cared about to each other helped me to cope with my own screwed up reality. I wasn't sure what was real and what was an illusion. My reality was tainted and obscure. I listened to the expected resistance from my son, who thought having his DNA in the system was nothing short of some government plot. I told him I thought he was funny, and I laughed. I told him if I had a grandchild out there somewhere he was hiding from me who wanted to locate family, this Bubby would not turn her grandbaby away. I went on to further point out that if he was a serial killer, the feds already had my DNA, so they'd hunt him down.

Agnes showed up on my Ancestry list of relatives and I was relieved. Of course, we could be first cousins according to the results. I continue to struggle with not having any full siblings. There are only half siblings. I was the youngest of five. Now I am one of seven. I am periodically notified that I have new relatives. Whenever I receive this email, I wonder if I am going to discover a new sister or brother. Aunt Rosie, who initially felt like my nemesis but ended up as someone I have really grown to adore, received a DNA kit for Christmas and appeared on my Ancestry account. Seeing my close connection to Aunt Rosie initially felt like a punch in the gut again. I was disappointed in myself because I thought I was over that. Aunt Rosie shares more DNA with me than Agnes, as does Aunt Charlene and my sister Rebecca. I don't call Rebecca my half-sister. Only the originals. Aren't I childish? It helps me cope. It makes me laugh when I think about it. As for Moshe, I haven't decided what to call him yet. I know the rejection is not about me, but I'm human and at times, it still feels personal.

As I was on shaky ground, especially in the beginning, I intuitively embarked on several endeavors to bring myself back to the earth. I called several of my high school friends. I called Sabatini, Bud, and Maryann. Sabatini and Bud are both full blooded Italian men who have been best friends ever since I can remember. Sabatini was tall, dark, and slim. He played the tall slim counterpart to lovable Bud. Sabatini was Felix and Bud was Oscar. Sabatini was Abbott and Bud was Costello. They did a rendition of "Who's on First" that my reunion group still reminisces about. Maryann is as Irish as Sabatini and Bud are Italian. Maryann is quick-witted, bright, well read and loyal.

My friend Lynne was already on board because we talk pretty frequently. Though she was not in high school with us, Lynne and I met at work when we waited tables at a pub when we were in our early thirties. We had two boys the same age, and we were moms and lonely wives with shared interests. Lynne believes she is an NPE too. There was a relative who slipped once who told her that her dad was not her biological father. She has never done her DNA and while her mom is still alive, she has elected not to open Pandora's Box. Each situation is unique.

I told each of my friends about my discovery. They all knew my parents. We grew up going to each other's house and spent many Saturday nights in front of the television watching Gilda Radner do Rosanne Rosanna Danna. I even called to tell my high school sweetheart. I told his brothers. It was random. I hadn't seen anyone in forty years or so. "Hi, blah blah, I haven't seen you in forty years! My dad is not my biological father." My nickname is Blurty. I sent each of them pictures of my biological father.

"I'm Jewish and Italian," I said to Sabatini.

"Yes, I see this! I see it! This is fantastic!!" was his reply.

Frankly, the only thing I found to be fantastic was the fact that I was still standing.

We made a date to go to dinner together as I wanted to make my new sister Rebecca the next debutante.

I believe my friends were all in shock. My parents were always so solid, for lack of a better term. I was raised in a secure, Roman Catholic home. My aunt was a nun, received most of the sacraments, first Friday mass, intact family. When I would get mouthy with my mom, she would retort, "Remember the fourth commandment of God!" If I only knew then what I know now, I would have made her elaborate on the rest of the command-ments.

We all met in a wonderful Italian restaurant in Moonachie, NJ. Jay was not with me this time. Sabatini, Budd, Maryann, and Lynne were all present. Rebecca and Jason were also with us.

Rebecca was nervous meeting all these new people that were my people. Once she warmed up, it would appear she was as happy as me. I wanted everyone to meet my sister. "Don't we look like sisters?" Rebecca asked all my friends several times. She asked on the way in, on the way out, and she asked Lynne in the bathroom. It was obvious that Rebecca was anxious. Maybe Rebecca needed validation too. I met her people. I wanted her to meet mine. I found it was extremely important to connect with my past. I wasn't sure if my present was real and when you first find out your DNA discovery, there is still that feeling that you have lived a lie your entire life. My past may not have been real, for all I knew. It is like being in the Twilight Zone. I had to give my friends hugs, and I metaphorically connected my past to my present. It was a seamless transition. They were all genuine, lovable individuals although I sprung this on my friends followed by veal parmigiana. I was Italian now, after all.

This time, it was my turn to make a toast. "I wish I could have known you sooner so I could have loved you longer." There. I said it. I used the L word. Using that L word was risky business. I was raised in a family where the last thing you did before you hung up the phone or left someone's house was tell them you loved them. It could have something to do with the possibility that you might never see that person again. I believe someone taught us all a script and the actors who played the parts were lousy performers. Actions speak louder than words and the words were incongruent with the actions of the individuals I called sisters and brother. How dramatic, how avant garde. "Love ya, love you, I love you, blah blah blah." There were no phone calls from my originals asking how I was handling the DNA discovery. They just kept sending me sister birthday cards which left me feeling empty and sad. My friends, new sister and her husband, and I enjoyed our dinner and created memories with each other. It was healing for me.

I reached out to a few other people to tell them my story. I called two maternal cousins who I am friends with on social media. My cousin is a writer, and she follows my blog. My one cousin stated, "Your dad was all about you." We had a conversation about how my dad was exceptional. Who raises another man's child and loves and cares so deeply? I was beyond fortunate.

"Did he know?" was the question everyone asked me.

"Yes, I believe he knew. I look just like my father and my dad knew him. He used to come to the house." I could tell my cousin was angry at my mother, but he said nothing. My other cousin talked about how people make mistakes. Once I figured everything out, I could forgive my mother. I felt there was a gamble in sharing my story because I did not want anyone taking pot shots at my mother. I felt like only I could do that.

"Well, the Publuski family were a group of partiers," my cousin said reminding me of our mothers' family. My other cousin listened and had the same reaction. He added, "None of us are angels." I knew all of this already and, to be honest, I must have needed to hear it. These two cousins are very close to my heart. I felt validated and accepted. "You were your dad's favorite." I smiled at this. I was his favorite, and he was mine. I heard some scuttlebutt about other family members talking about my business. Once the information gets out there, you have no control over who tells who. I heard another cousin of mine called Agnes to see what this DNA story was about. She never called me. Another cousin told me she heard it from my aunt. So, your experience may become fodder for gossip. Don't let that bother you. You have no control over it.

I reached out to my paternal cousin, Dee, which was scary for me. I waited until the last paternal aunt died. I didn't want to hurt anyone or explain myself if I didn't have to. She was the sister of the self-proclaimed family genealogist.

"Dee," I said, "I have something to tell you. My dad was not my biological father."

I went through the entire story with her over the phone. Dee listened intently to the full story. She then announced how impressed she was that my parents stayed together despite my mother's infidelity. What followed was something that was touching and heartwarming.

Dee said, "It doesn't matter to me who your biological father was. You are still my cousin. It doesn't change anything." I was relieved. I felt supported. I felt loved. Of course, after we hung up the phone, I cried again. I had to drink a lot of water to replace the tears I shed.

I told my adult children early on. Nobody openly expressed anything negative except Matthew exclaimed what I was feeling, "Your whole life was a lie, mom." My three kids absolutely adored my mom and dad. I still wanted my three kids to meet my new family. After all, they shared from the same set of biological roots that I now call my own. The first to make the connection was my youngest son. During my trip up north, we had him meet us in my hometown in Bergen County. We all went to Bruno's Pizza. He had a chance to really talk with Rebecca and Jason.

"This is your nephew Matthew, Rebecca." Matt had his girlfriend with him, and Rebecca was welcoming and friendly. It was the first time I met Matthew's girlfriend, too.

Matthew was quite the chatterbox. He was so overcome with happiness over finding out he was Sicilian! It was comical to listen to him. We ate New Jersey pizza (the pizza in Florida sucks), laughed and shared stories. On the way, we took pictures of us together to chronicle our new adventure. Matthew hurried home to call his older brother Buzz. "Buzz," he said, "We are related to the Sopranos."

6

THE GREEN EYE CLUB
& HAMANTASCHEN

"Once you're into this family, there's no getting out."
—Tony Soprano

I grew up around a lot of Italians, as most of my neighborhood smelled like gravy on a Sunday afternoon. Most of our neighbors had kitchens in their basements and Mrs. Lovigina made the best pizza I ever had. I dated an Italian in high school for a few years, my godmother was Italian, and all my closest friends seemed to have Italian last names. My skin turned dark in the summers and often people would ask me if I was Italian, to which I always answered no. I would proudly counter, "I am Polish, Swedish, French, and English." It never bothered me. I just always wondered how these people could guess Italian. I have dark hair and light eyes. The dark hair always made sense, but the light eyes never screamed Italian. My neighbors all had brown eyes. I met many northern Italians who had the lightest blue-green eyes I had ever seen. This was apparently the case with my biological father's family. Aunt Lori told me that most of the Barrie family has light eyes.

When I first told Buzz about our recently revealed Italian

ethnicity, he quickly replied, in between text messaging friends, "That's why you always made such great sauce."

"Let's get one thing straight, Buzz," I quickly countered, "It's gravy."

As for being Jewish, well, since the wasband was Jewish, my children carry that gene and Buzz and I continue to engage in playful bantering about whether being Jewish is a religion, a culture, or an ethnicity. He always must have the last word which I always have to let him have. I explain tirelessly that being Jewish to some is a religion, nationality, and culture. Hitler didn't care what you believed it was. I tried to bring some of the culture into our home while the kids were growing up, since their father is Jewish. I seemed to care more about it than he did, our Hanukkahs were short-lived. It is not clear to me why things like culture and religion were not part of my former husband's repertoire. That was such a long time ago. But it was too much for me to take care of both Christian and Jewish traditions at the time. His grand-mother made me hamantaschen every Purim, and she slipped and called me a "dirty gentile" once. Grandma caught herself because I laughed so hard, she turned beet red and apologized for the next hour. Of course, I teased her for that entire hour. If she only knew that I actually was part of her tribe.

One of the first things I did in the month or two after my DNA discovery was search out information on being Jewish. I was raised as a good Catholic girl, and I felt somewhat unique that I was carrying the same ethnicity as Jesus. I looked up Jews for Jesus and researched Messianic Judaism. I barely composed myself, speaking with and asking a million questions to a Messianic Jewish therapist I worked with at the hospital, and he gave me his phone number in case I had more questions. I found a Jewish group online that scheduled a community Passover meal. I was bound and determined to see for myself what being Jewish meant to me. Jay and two of our friends made plans to attend my first official Passover meal as a brand-new Jewish woman. Processing all of this and learning was no simple task. To some, Judaism is an ethnic religion steeped in both cultural and religious tradition. To others, the focus seems to be on culture. There are Jewish families who have Christmas trees and celebrate the holiday in its secular form. In the DNA companies, 23andMe and Ancestry both initially labeled the genetic characteristic I found as Ashkenazi Jewish and recently, Ancestry changed its label to, "Jewish Peoples of Europe." Sometimes I still have difficulty wrapping my head around the whole thing as I struggle to find my personal meaning for all of this. So far, my delight in unearthing this finding is feeling a stronger shared connection to my children.

We were welcomed at the garage door at a home in Spring Hill, Florida. All the men were wearing dark black clothes. They studied the four of us curiously. I suppose the head rabbi is the person who approached. I knew I was not to offer my hand as I was clearly with individual Orthodox Jewish men. The women were all inside the home preparing for Passover.

"What brought you here?" asked the curious rabbi.

"I just found out I am Jewish, and I would like to learn more."

I introduced Jay and our young friends, Sarah and Rob. Jay came because I made him come. He did not have a choice in the matter.

"I just found out that my father was half Jewish and that his father converted," I continued.

"Your father and not your mother?" countered the rabbi.

I was beyond floored by the rabbi's response.

"You are not Jewish," he said.

I felt a knot in my throat, and I wanted to run for the hills. I didn't cry, but I wanted to. I don't know how I contained myself. Jay told me later he wanted to leave with the way the rabbi was talking to me. Hey, if I can handle Aunt Rosie, I can handle this guy. We proceeded inside. The rabbi had a lovely wife who began talking with me like I knew what I was doing. She offered to have me light some special candles, and I noticed the kitchen was bright and cheery. Several of her children were intently studying the adults in the room, especially the strange new ones. It was tense for the first forty-five minutes. Finally, we sat down to dinner with a reformed rabbi who was visiting for Passover. He invited us to his temple and thought we might be more comfortable there.

It was a long four hours. The lead rabbi's father was in attendance, and he commented that nobody left. I was told later that people don't stay for the entire dinner. I fought the urge to say at least I was respectful. I wanted to tell him that my parents raised me well, and I thought it would be rude to leave an event that felt sacred on so many levels. Several of my Jewish friends asked why on earth I would choose an Orthodox Seder to explore on my first try, for my first Passover. It ruined Jay from going to any other Passover celebrations. He still hasn't forgiven me. I related the Passover Seder to New Testament readings of the Last Supper and the celebration of communion I participated in every Sunday growing up. I found the whole thing to be fascinating. My favorite part of the Seder (aside from watching our friend being offered fish he wouldn't eat on a bet) was the way the rabbi blessed the food and said, "Blessed are you, O God, our Lord, King of the Universe…" I always found that start of a prayer to be an exquisite way to honor God. In eighth grade I won the religion award. I think I would have made a pretty good Jew if I chose to.

Now it was time for another visit with Aunt Charlene. My lovely baker aunt planned a day of hamantaschen baking because I told her I loved those cookies. What went along with that was that I introduced my daughter Noel into the tribe. Another surprise was presented as I checked in to my hotel room. I was advised that Aunt Rosie was planning on coming. I was terrified now and worried since I did not pack an asbestos suit. The phone call from Rebecca with this news was amusing as Bubbles (my nickname for Rebecca because I told her she was effervescent) did not disappoint with the level of anxiety she created (all in fun) and something we can still giggle about.

Noel and I drove up from the New Jersey shore in the morning, making idle conversation about what to expect. I told her all about how lovely Aunt Charlene was and about the family I had met so far. Noel was sneezing all the way up the parkway. I think she was nervous because she didn't have a cold. We never really spoke about how she was feeling. She followed my blog, AncestryDiscoveries.com, so Noel was not a stranger to all that I had gone through.

Prior to the trip, I pulled out baby pictures of Noel. She was fair haired with striking green eyes. I compared the same fair-haired, green-eyed picture of my sister Rebecca. The two looked an awful lot alike.

We arrived at Aunt Charlene's and Rebecca met us there. Aunt Charlene gave us all big hugs and ushered us into the kitchen where there was cookie dough ready to roll. We all jumped right in. Rebecca doesn't bake, so she stayed in the other room with Lyndsey, who doesn't bake either. I think they were happy I joined the family so that Aunt Charlene had someone to share her recipes with. Aunt Charlene told me she invited Aunt Rosie, who was going to be driven by her son Vic with his wife Anna. That would be another new cousin that I got to meet, and I was happy about that. Vic is the first grandchild and the first male. I am the first granddaughter of my grandmother.

We were rolling right along when there were three faces standing in the window of the screen door, peering through the glass and knocking. The moment of truth had arrived. The fourth member of our green-eyed party was about to make her debut. I never saw so many green-eyed people in my life. We were all in one room. I had a resemblance to Noel, Rebecca, and now I could see that Aunt Rosie and I looked alike, too. For fifty-seven years, I never looked like anyone except my offspring. Now the numbers were increasing. It was utterly amazing.

The infamous Aunt Rosie entered the room and my heart stood still. Would she hug me or hit me with her pocketbook? Aunt Rosie stood six inches away from me. "Nice to meet you," she said. "Nice to meet you too," I replied. "This is my daughter, Noel. She is your grandniece." Aunt Rosie eyed her too, and they exchanged cordiality. My stomach was nervous, but I was still enjoying the moment. I took lots of pictures. My cousin Vic, Aunt Rosie's son, and his wife, Anna, were lovely individuals. Vic was retired, and the two did a great deal of traveling. We talked about some future travel, perhaps to Florida.

My nervous energy turned into productivity which translated into Noel and I pumping out hamantaschen at the speed of Lucy and Ethel wrapping candy in the candy factory. The centers of the cookies had apricots, strawberries, dates, and sesame seeds. After the treats were cooling, we all sat in the living room, and I listened to stories of my biological father from Aunt Rosie. She went into that pocketbook she did not hit me with and pulled out a little package wrapped in a paper towel. It was a refrigerator magnet that was made of finished wood. The words inscribed were, "Women run for office, not coffee." Pocono Mts, PA.

"Your father gave me this, Alexandra. I wanted you to have it." My biological father was a politician. When I was digging deeper to find out who this man was, I found countless articles about the numerous times he ran for office. Aunt Rosie worked for a New Jersey politician and she herself ran for congress at some point. Aunt Rosie had such an enriching past with politics, activism, and travel. She and her husband traveled the world. Ironically, they lived in the same town I worked in those summers with my mother. We ate at the same café, The Daily Treat, on East Ridgewood Ave. My family was right in front of me, and I never knew it.

Aunt Charlene had a feast on her dining room table. I had yet another moment in time that is etched into my biological fibers. You could never understand it if you haven't experienced it. This green eye club party/cookie bake was monumental to me and there was one of the first of many profound moments that continue to this day.

I took plenty of pictures the day of the green-eye-club party so that I could make more collages of my new family side by side with my kids, to see the generational resemblance. That resemblance goes beyond looks and seeps into character. I made copies of those pictures for everyone and to this day, Aunt Charlene's picture wearing a red and white checked apron with ruffles standing in front of one of her Kitchen Aids framed in gold, hangs in a designated place of honor in my kitchen. Her daughter Lyndsey has the same picture framed in her office. Aunt Rosie says I captured Aunt Charlene's essence. I made sure everyone in the family got a copy of Aunt Charlene's picture. A happy but confused woman returned to Florida. I was happy because I found my tribe. I felt content and validated because after Aunt Rosie took in our festivities the day before leaving, she smiled, hugged me, and said, "Now I know what your goal was." My confusion was in what I felt about my mom and dad, Irene and Lou, and what they would have to say about this reunion with my kin. I felt like I was cheating on Lou.

After I was home for several days, another surprise happened. Aunt Lori called me out of the blue, "I would really like to get to know you." We talked for hours. Prior to moving to Florida, Aunt Lori lived one town away from me in Ocean County, NJ and her son, Bill, told me he thought we looked like twins. I never met Bill, but we are friends on social media. This is the case for most of my new family, except for the elusive Moshe. Aunt Lori and I talked about her work in behavioral health facilities and mine in private practice. In several months, I could pay her a visit, as I had planned another trip up north for a business event.

I flew into Atlantic City, NJ in a cold November. I missed the snow by two days so there was just enough on the ground to be safe enough to drive, satisfy the "isn't this pretty" followed by,

"It's too cold here. I want to go home to Florida." When I closed my NJ practice, I still maintained some of my clients through telehealth, and certainly my relationships. I signed on to go to a "Beef and Brew" fundraiser with a group called, "New Horizons" based in Pennsylvania, not too far from Philadelphia. I made this trip without Jay, who was always happy to avoid the winter at all costs. Jay knew I made plans with Aunt Lori and her wife, Aunt Samantha, who were eager to see what I looked like. By this time, I was a relative. It was clear I was not a fortune hunter. Connection was healing; connection brought me a degree of peace that was severely lacking after my discovery.

The next morning, I packed up my bag and drove back to New Jersey to meet another new aunt. I picked up a bottle of wine as I was invited to Aunt Lori and Aunt Samantha's home for lunch. By this time, the aunts had already decided that I was to call them aunt and I was regularly corrected a few times if I left out the "aunt" title. I was nervous, but not as nervous as when I met Aunt Rosie.

"Breathe in, breathe out," I told myself. I rang the doorbell and was met by two pleasant, curious women in their early seventies. Aunt Lori looks exactly like Rebecca. I resemble both. Aunt Lori cries a little and touches my face. She gives me the warmest hug. Aunt Lori is wearing high heels. I gave those up ten years ago. I am wondering how she is walking in them. Since I have met most of the family, we have something to talk about. Aunt Lori and I move into her sunroom, and we have a glass of wine. We talk about what it is like to live in Ocean County, New Jersey. We touch on politics (my least favorite topic) and how my experience is going. Aunt Lori has green eyes too. She tells me stories about my grandmother which I love hearing. She talks to me about my father. My aunts prepared a lovely lunch, and we sat around the table talking for hours.

Aunt Samantha wanted to hear how all went with Aunt Rosie, who I have learned has a reputation for being a straightforward, no-nonsense, tell it like it is kinda gal. "Well," I said, "When I first spoke to Aunt Rosie, she told me I created quite the stir in this family." Aunt Samantha was smiling ear to ear. I continued, "And I said to Aunt Rosie, 'I beg to differ with you ma'am, but I am not the one who created the stir.'"

"You said that to Aunt Rosie?" Aunt Samantha smirked. Her silence said it all. Aunt Rosie is a firecracker, even at the tender age of ninety something. I believe I am a lot like her, and the apple does not fall far from the family genetic tree. Though I don't want to rush my life, its entertaining to imagine myself at her age, raising hell and being brutally honest. Aunt Samantha stared at my short hair from across the table and said, "Lori, I think you should get your hair cut short again." Wow, I suppose I bear a strong resemblance to Aunt Lori.

Aunt Lori talked with me about Aunt Rosie. She told me she has explored this new discovery with Aunt Rosie in great depth. Aunt Lori uses the word "explore" frequently and I am sure it is an occupational hazard because that is a word we regularly use in therapy. She shares that Aunt Rosie would like to spend time with me alone. I can feel my stomach knotting up. Receiving all this preparation for spending time alone with Aunt Rosie was not as bad as it seems. The first time was the hardest. Once I realized how similar I was to Aunt Rosie, it took the jitters away. Aunt Rosie tells it like it is, which is an apparent family trait that Aunt Rosie excels at.

My next trip up north was soon planned. I knew that Aunt Rosie would be part of that trip. My trips up to New Jersey to get to know my new family were frequent during the first two years. I spent most of my time getting to know Rebecca. For each day spent with other family members, I spent two or three with Rebecca doing sisterly things like shopping or hanging out, spending time in her living room playing with the dog and talking. I was writing the whole time through all of this newly discovered family experience, to process what I was feeling.

With each trip, I would email Moshe, to no avail. His wife sent me a friend request on social media, and I accepted. Rebecca forwarded copies of texts to me from Moshe's wife, reporting that Moshe finally agreed to meet me. It seemed Rebecca was pretty excited, too. The so-called meeting never took place. It was like having an elusive brother carrot dangled in front of my nose that was always a few towns out of reach. I finally stopped sending emails and disconnected from his wife during one of those trips when he had a bar mitzvah planned for his son. He and his wife refused to see me (the communication came from her) because they were busy with bar mitzvah planning and "people are coming from all over the world." She sent me family pictures, but the entire scene was too painful, and I had to protect myself. I couldn't go from one family of being excluded into another. Except for one slip up wishing Moshe and his family a Merry Christmas, I gave up.

I flew up during early December 2019 to spend time with Rebecca for Christmas and made plans with Aunt Rosie. Aunt Rosie wanted to go to her favorite Italian restaurant, "Nanni's" in Rochelle Park, NJ. I picked her up at her apartment. Vic and Anna could not make it that day, so it was going to be just the two of us. Aunt Rosie and I talked for hours over antipasti and scrumptious Italian specialties. She told me all about the origin of the restaurant and the staff treated us like royalty. Aunt Rosie sure shined. After lunch, we walked through the halls of her senior apartment building. She introduced me to the other residents proudly, "This is my niece." She talked to one of the elderly ladies, saying, "Let's get together after the holiday and get into trouble. It will be so much fun." I used to tell my college roommates the same thing: "We'll get into so much trouble; it will be so much fun." It's in the genes. Can you tell I adore Aunt Rosie?

I spent the whole day with my aunt. Rebecca was texting me intermittently to make sure my body was still intact. I assured her I was fine. Aunt Rosie and I are kindred spirits of sorts. Before

I left, she threw her arms around me and said, "I so enjoyed today. I am glad it was just us. I am so glad you came. Now, when are you coming back?"

I have so much more love in my life than I ever thought possible. Aunt Rosie moved into an assisted living facility in early January after our first solo visit. I saw her once before the world shut down and made subsequent visits when things opened up again. We talk every few weeks to catch up with life. Aunt Rosie is the mayor of her assisted living facility, head of the resident's counsel, and chief participator in all activities. During my last visit, Jay came along at Aunt Rosie's request since she had never met him. We spent the better part of two days on a heartwarming, gracious visit with her at her facility. Our smile muscles hurt from the laughter. Aunt Rosie endearingly shared serious and comical family stories and she was beyond jovial, chuckling at some of her own behaviors. She has an index finger she points at people when she is making a serious point that her family calls, "Ed." Aunt Rosie laughed at that too. It was beyond special to honor her for her ninety-second birthday with a requested visit.

Previously, during Covid when travel was much lighter, I made the trip up to North Jersey to see Aunt Charlene and Aunt Rosie. Aunt Charlene was sick. Aunt Lori called me almost daily to give me updates. I was touched by her compassion as she said to me, "I think you should know." I would receive my daily updates and I had to decide, should I go see my new Aunt Charlene before she leaves the earth or is it not the right thing to do? There are no books written on the subject and I followed my heart. There were plans being made for Aunt Charlene to be moved to the hospice from the hospital. While she was in the hospital, I sent Aunt Charlene flowers so she could enjoy them. We talked on the phone several times before she became too weak.

Aunt Charlene, not knowing I was in the loop about her failing condition, asked me, "When are you coming again? Come soon." I was teetering back-and-forth in my thought process. Should I go now or wait until there was a funeral?

L'chaim! To life! was my usual MO, even before I found out I was Jewish. My mom used to say, "Life is for the living." The trip was planned, and my friend Lynne picked me up from the airport. We were lunching with Aunt Rosie that afternoon and the plan was to see Aunt Charlene the next day. During lunch, I received a text message that Aunt Charlene was being moved to hospice in a day or two. I broke the news to Aunt Rosie after lunch. She was shocked and sad. Hopefully, there would still be an opportunity for me to see Aunt Charlene.

We always seem to eat when I go to New Jersey, so in the spirit of my sojourns up north, Lynne and I went to Rebecca's for pizza, my favorite food, especially when I go back home. It gave Lynne and Rebecca a chance to chat. Lynne went home that night, and Rebecca and I made plans to go to the Meadowlands flea market the following day.

Saturday morning, Rebecca and I strolled the flea market while I waited to hear I was clear for a hospital visit. Rebecca ended up joining me in our schlep to Hackensack Hospital. She was happy that she did. We both could say our goodbyes together.

Aunt Charlene recognized us when we walked into her room. She was pale and appeared frail. She announced to me, "Frank is going to help me from here." Frank was my deceased biological father's name. "Keith and Jerry are going to help me, too." Keith and Jerry were the names of my deceased first cousins, Aunt Charlene's two sons.

Rebecca and I got a bit choked up. I didn't know what to say, so I said what I felt.

"Please tell Frank I say hello."

A young, petite Asian doctor entered the room. Are you both family members? I am speechless. This was a surreal moment. There I was, feeling clueless, and I probably looked like a deer in the headlights in this moment. Do I count as family? Rebecca saved the day and answered in the affirmative. We were whisked to a private room by the doctor, who had questions about a move to hospice. I gave the doctor the report on Aunt Charlene's visits with my biological father and her sons. The doctor then said, perhaps she could not decide. I assured the doctor that Aunt Charlene knew who we were and that I was under the opinion that it was close to the end. Many times, before people die, they see loved ones who were previously deceased. I told the doctor I was a therapist. Rebecca and I let the doctor know that Aunt Charlene's children were on their way and that they would make whatever decisions were necessary. We stayed for a bit, holding Aunt Charlene's hands, and speaking softly. My cousin Lyndsey texted that her brother was there, and it was his turn to visit his mom. Before we left, I whispered in Aunt Charlene's ear, "Thank you for everything. I love you."

Aunt Charlene died the day I left. I did not find out until I was back at home in Florida. I was so happy I got to say goodbye.

7

METAPHYSICS, MYSTICS, & PAST LIFE REGRESSIONS

"Death ends a life, not a relationship."
—Mitch Albom

I endured nine years of Catholic school and witnessed my share of abusive nuns. We all laugh about it now, but it cost me some time in therapy. Don't get me wrong, I don't hate nuns. I had to overcome my own prejudices because when I take inventory, there have been several of these brides of Christ who have been a very productive and loving part of my life. No matter what happened, I prayed my way through it. You know something? Prayer works. My experiences led me to explore other faith traditions and all of this exploration leads me back to a strong faith I have had my whole life. Two of the teachings I have learned are that psychic mediums are off limits and there is no such thing as reincarnation. Well, from my support groups, I learned that many of us go to psychics since our parents are no longer around to answer questions and our original families are sometimes uncooperative, or they don't have the answers either. The intention is to discover the truth. Some of us went beyond our own belief system to get to the elusive truth. There was no plan to dishonor God. After all, God has been a co-pilot throughout the entire journey.

Here's the inherent problem in all of this. Over the last several years, I read about near-death experiences and had one myself at two and a half. It was a profound experience, to say the least, and one which left behind indescribable feelings of peace and love. Like my DNA discovery, I have come out of the closet with this experience. If sharing my encounter with the other side helps bring peace to someone else, I would share it. I read books by Baptists who share their discovery of life after death, having had near-death experiences themselves. Somehow, the rule about talking to dead people or not has not been a worry of mine. Past life regressions might be viewed in two ways. The first is that it actually is a past life. The second is that you are experiencing your own story from another dimension in a dream state, which leaves this moment in time open to metaphorical interpretation. During hypnosis, most therapists will take you into several regressions. Sometimes returning to the past is most likely an age regression, but sometimes, an actual past life regression appears to happen. I leave the interpretation up to my clients. I wanted answers, like so many NPEs. Similar to so many of my NPE colleagues, my loved ones with the answers are all deceased. Others have reported that they explored spiritual possibilities and I too searched out psychic mediums to help me put the pieces together of my life's pattern, which seems to shape up but has not been sewn together yet. I was regressed to the womb twice and both times my experience was the same. The first time was perplexing and made no sense, until my discovery.

My mother is dead, my dad is dead, and my biological father is dead. I needed to understand what their connection was on some level and how they felt about what transpired and what continues to develop in my present ride on this roller coaster we call the NPE experience. I have always been one to meditate to relax my mind. I have a somewhat stressful job as a psychotherapist and my life has been very stressful, though not that different from most people. Having been trained as a heart-centered hypnotherapist, I am familiar with the deep relaxation that a hypnotic trance offers. When I first embarked on my DNA journey, I turned inward first. I knew from reading and attending some workshops on metaphysics that you did not need a medium to talk to dead people. Sounds strange, doesn't it? But if I connected with someone so intimately throughout my life, why would death be any different? Love never dies. It just changes form.

My dad Lou and I had been close from the time I can remember. When my mother had difficulty connecting to me, Lou never wavered. I believe my dad knew I was Frank's biological daughter. I am Frank's female clone. My dad Lou was a kind, gentle soul who never had a bad word to say about anyone. He had a marvelous sense of humor. He was my first known parent who died, and I can recall every sad detail of what that experience was like for me and for my children. Losing my dad bred some of the most sorrowful feelings I had ever known. My dad expressed concerns about dying around my children before we ever moved in together. He did not want the kids to suffer loss, which is inevitable when there is love. It is part of the package. Time together was worth every tear shed.

My dad told me that when Buzz was born, he had a dream that I was standing in his doorway. There was a bright light behind me, and I told him it was time for me to have the baby. Buzz was born around 4:30am on Black Friday and nobody knew we left for the hospital. My dad knew.

Prior to his death, my dad made several ambulance trips to the hospital over the years. On one occasion, after spending several hours with him, I went home for the evening. I had a nagging feeling. There was a little voice inside of me that told me to go back to the hospital and to go back NOW. I followed my intuition. I drove back to the hospital. In those days, security was not as tight as it is now. I ventured up to the fourth floor. I found my dad alone and projectile vomiting while his call button was lying on the tiled floor. In a gravelly voice, he choked, "Get an orderly." I rushed to the nurses' station in a panic where the night nurses were shocked to see me. I gave them hell. It took several days for the vomiting to stop. I knew.

I was attending a meeting on July 22, 2002, in South Toms River, NJ. I looked at my watch and reported to everyone in the room that I had "time to go give my father a kiss." Immediately, I headed for the hospital, joining my mom and Agnes. My mom and Agnes kissed my dad. I kissed him. I waited in the hall and sat on a chair. My mom and Agnes left the hospital. I felt compelled to give my dad another kiss before I left. I whispered in his good ear that I was leaving my angels with him, and he said with his eyes closed, "I feel them." I went home to cook dinner. I received a phone call from Agnes a short time later that my dad, Lou, died. We both knew. My friend Pastor Joe, told me that what my dad and I both experienced was dying grace.

The first person I desperately wanted to talk to was my dad when I uncovered this horrendous white lie. The day I made this discovery, I longed to cry in my dad's arms. I wanted him to say, "Kid, it's going to be okay." I was feeling like a traitorous, ungrateful daughter for pursuing the truth of my biological paternal tribe. Was I just supposed to keep living the lie and pretending I never took a DNA test? So, I thought I would try to reach out on a spiritual level to my dad minus the medium I didn't need in order to do that. Connection is a spiritual experience. Since my dad and I had that bond in life, I thought it was worth a try to communicate with him directly. I was getting ready for bed. My husband was already breathing heavily and snuggled in for the night. I said a prayer of protection.

I had gone to my dad in this dreamlike state many times before when I needed comfort or advice. I never needed my dad more than I needed him now. Lou appeared wearing his old-fashioned shiny brown and white buttoned shoes in my mind's eye. Dressed to the nines, he had on a dark brown pinstripe suit, and he was in his early forties. He gently touched the side of my face and his brown eyes gazed into mine. It is as though he could feel the sadness, the grief, the longing to have all these tears that persistently caused my eyes to swell washed away. He only spoke a few words:

"Alexandra, it doesn't change a thing between us."

It felt like my dad was right there in the room with me. I couldn't say a word as I began to uncontrollably weep, feeling sad because he was not in the flesh but relieved at the same time. I held on to those words for the last four years, sometimes wondering if I really had that connection from beyond the veil. Recently, in my sleeping dream state without me asking, my dad visited me again.

"Alexandra," he said, "It doesn't change a thing between us. You belong to me."

This time, because I had four plus years to process my original experience, the opportunity existed now for me to reply.

"Daddy, I know. I want you to know that I love you and you are extraordinary."

I cried so hard I woke myself up. This meeting experience was as real as the first one. It was validating. So much had happened and I had the sense that my dad, Lou, was traveling along with me through the entire ordeal. He knew I was not biologically his. He had to have known. When I turned fourteen, my dad gave me a ring. He let me pick it out. It was a beautiful ring and I still have it. Who gives their daughter a ring? I have only seen lovers exchange rings. Rings mean, "You belong to me." They also can mean, "Somebody wants me." I believe that ring was my dad's way of saying that I was his, no matter what the DNA said.

You can imagine my surprise at a serendipitous event that followed forty-seven years after I received that ring from my dad. It was my birthday gift. Jay and I were visiting with my Aunt Lori and Aunt Samantha. After a delicious Italian dinner, we returned to their home for dessert. Jay and I got lost on the way to their home. We were at a stop sign and we saw twenty deer sitting on someone's lawn. Out came the cameras. The deer were leading the way. We found their house and were ushered in making ourselves at home on comfy chairs. Aunt Lori returned from the other room with a gift bag. I carefully unwrapped a small box. Within was a beautiful amethyst ring. People who believe in the healing power of crystals and stones know amethyst is a catalyst for healing. Apparently my father, Frank, gave this ring to his mother. Aunt Lori, someone who attributes meaning to just about everything, wanted me to have the ring because it indirectly came from my father. Two rings, two fathers who I am connected to. One loved me enough to raise me and care for me, and one loved me enough to let me go. The spiritual exploration continued.

I engaged in paranormal communication through several spiritual mediums. Bobby, Blair Robertson, John Edward, and Blair again. I was regressed by Brian Weiss, MD twice. The first time was on a voice recording. The second was in person when I took his class at the Omega Institute in Rhinebeck, NY.

Bobby the psychic medium

Somewhere in between detailed genograms and hours of research, I consulted directly with a medium to see exactly what my biological father knew. It was not a pleasant experience and it only left me with more questions. Something didn't feel right. The medium had so many issues of his own, which he projected onto me. I had a picture of my biological father as a sperm donor in a leisure suit and in the beginning, I even called him Leisure Suit Larry the Lounge Lizard. He was handsome in my mind's eye and distinguished with a martini glass in his hand. All of this wasn't true. I have since come to learn more about him. Depending on who I speak to, I hear Frank was funny, outspoken, and he struggled with depression, which seemed to lead to alcoholism.

Frank married a woman a few years after his discreet relationship with my mother. I have since learned that Frank had several affairs with married women. All were businesswomen. After a few drinks, he would call their spouse to let them know. Before he died, he involved himself with a married businesswoman who left her husband for him. It seems like this was a pattern Frank followed. In the end, it seems like he may have gotten what he wanted. In his last relationship, the woman left her husband for him. I learned to trust my intuition from consulting with this medium. I knew someone would come along eventually who would provide me with paranormal information. Not clear how much of the above is from Bobby.

Blair Robertson, the psychic medium

Blair is a psychic medium from Canada. He was having a gallery event in Tampa. I coaxed Jay to go with me. The entire week before, I spoke with my mother. I spoke while I was driving. I talked to her whenever I was alone. She never answered back. I asked her to please come through, as I needed to hear from her. I nagged her in the morning, I nagged her in between client sessions, I was persistent. Lo and behold, the night comes along and there are over two hundred people in the room.

In walks Blair. He has a tropical shirt on, and he likes to cuss. He forewarned all his onlookers that he had language that matched his colorful tropical shirt. We all laugh. I sat through the first several readings and I was silently talking to my mother, nagging again. She owed me an explanation after all I had gone through. I was beyond betrayed by the secret she never shared.

"I am seeing a woman skipping through. She is dropping F bombs," Blair announced.

Yep, that's my mother. Her favorite phrase was, "You ain't so mucken fuch." It took me a few years to figure out what that meant, like forty years. I'm a little slow on the uptake with sarcasm.

He went on to say, "She is showing me two families. One family has five kids and one with three. You are part of both families."

I knew this was me. I was the last of five kids and now the eldest of three.

Blair had Jay and I stand and someone rushed over with a microphone as though we were on the Donohue show.

Blair offered a slew of information about my mother. He talked about her crocheting doilies and afghans. My mother and I had a private joke about doilies. She tried to teach me to crochet. Every single time I tried to make a granny square, it looked like a doily. It had to be mom. Blair kept going and described more details. He then mentioned that she had a secret and she had something she wanted to tell me. I held my breath.

"Your mom says she is sorry," he announced to the room of people disappointed he hadn't called on them.

He looked at me quite puzzled. He had no clue what she was talking about. I knew. I don't believe my mother was sorry I was born. I believe she was sorry for the pain associated with my DNA discovery. At the time of this reading, I was in deep grief. I am sure there was no intent to cause pain, not from any of my three parents. There was no DNA sixty years ago and adoptions happened in secret. If a woman announced she was pregnant, she was in jeopardy of losing her job whether she was single or married. I remember my mom sharing that her boss did not like the fact that she was pregnant. She had to wear baggy clothing and was moved to the back of the office. It even happened thirty-seven years ago to me when an airline reneged on a job offer they made to me when I told them I was pregnant. There was no safe abortion sixty years ago. In hindsight, it was a blessing that the airline job fell through, but that would not have happened today. Life has changed, and the world is so much more litigious. What about my right to know? Was I being protected? Who else was being protected? Like most ethical dilemmas, there were too many gray areas to consider.

Blair then asked, "How have you experienced healing from this?"

I cried into the microphone, "I had hoped my mom would come through and apologize."

There was thunderous applause. I had set my sights on being read. I wanted to hear from my mother. My task was to work on forgiving her. My mom was human and made mistakes. It is tough when you figure out that your parents are not perfect, i.e. human. My mother was telling me she empathized with my pain. While I was growing up, she battled demons I thought were my fault. She reconciled her demons within herself by the time I was in my late teens. Now, she seemed to hope I could exorcise the demons that were haunting me.

John Edward, the psychic medium

Months passed, and I had it in my head that I wanted to hear from my biological father. Lo and behold, an advertisement came across my cyber desk on social media. John Edward, a well-known psychic medium, was on his way to Tampa! It was a few months prior to the pandemic. I tried again. This time, I was talking to my father, Frank. I told him I wanted to hear from him. I needed to hear from him. A colleague told me she loved John Edward and used to rush home from school to watch his television show. Event tickets make the perfect gift, after all, so Jessica, my colleague, joined us. When there are messages coming through from mediums, healing occurs for others, too. I was preparing myself. My bio father was being prepared by me. I started nagging him as I had nagged my mother a week before the event. One can only wonder what people thought when they saw me in the car talking to myself. "Frank, you owe me this – I want John Edward to relay a message from you. It would be great to know all the details of your relationship with my mother." Jay and I had seen John Edward before. I only practiced my newfound spiritual technique of badgering spirits because of my DNA discovery. One good turn deserves another and I have been haunted by my parents' indiscretion. It was only fair that I reciprocate.

This time the room was larger, with approximately five-hundred people. We waited patiently for the show to begin. Out came John Edward, as big as life. Our seats were only slightly off to the side. The lighting and the acoustics were much better than the first time we went to a reading. John was off to our right and the readings began. I started to silently pester Frank to get John over to our side of the room.

Lo and behold, here he comes! Then he calls on the party right next to us. Damn, I think that he'd never read both of us. We were sitting too close together.

"And someone who passed donated their organs to science," said John Edward.

"No," the group next to us said in unison, looking at each other.

I raised my hand. He WAS on our side of the room. He WAS about to read us!

Here comes the microphone. We were on Donohue yet another time. Give me that thing. It was as though Miss America was disqualified and I was the first runner-up moving in to snag the crown I deserved.

The three of us stood up. I am shaking on the inside.

"My best friend in high school died last year on my birthday," I offered. "She donated all of her organs to science."

Touchdown! Would it be too obvious if I started high fiving Jay and my co-worker?

"I am also seeing two men standing together with a woman. The woman feels like a mother figure. Did your mother pass?" asked John.

"Yes," I replied. You are not supposed to give the mediums any information.

"The two men both feel like father figures for me." John Edward looked puzzled again.

"That's because I have two fathers," I answered. People were shuffling uncomfortably in their seats a little.

I continued, "I did a DNA test and found out that my dad was not my biological father." The audience sighed.

John Edward continued, "Why am I connecting you to the Unabomber?" He was smiling in disbelief. Maybe he thought one of my fathers was a murderer or something.

"Oh, because I dated a serial killer," I said.

(During college, I dated a handsome man who ended up working for a well-known computer firm. There is a true crime book written about him.)

The audience broke out into hysterics. Everyone was laughing. It was surreal and a little warped, but as I am a little warped myself, I laughed too.

John Edward went on, "How many women did he kill?"

"Two for sure, and he is suspected of another murder. He invited me upstairs for a cup of coffee the last time I saw him, but I didn't go." The audience is practically rolling on the floor. I am not trying to be funny, but I guess my tone was matter-of-fact. Doesn't everyone date a serial killer at least once in their life?

"I think you had a guardian angel protecting you," said John Edward.

"I think I had a legion of angels protecting me," I replied. More laughter from the audience.

John Edward went back to my mother and fathers.

"How do you feel about your mother in all of this?" he asked.

I looked out at the audience and smiled. "I forgive my mother."

I needed to say that to five hundred people and be heard. It was true at that point. It had been just over two years. I turned a corner there. I felt better.

"This was the dad that raised you coming through," he said.

Somehow, I felt like it had to be Frank and not Lou. He was the one who I hassled all week in my spare time. Besides, I didn't need a medium to talk to my dad.

John Edward read Jay. I had felt guilty that I kept getting readings. Every time we go to one of these events, the readings would center on me. I was hoping John Edward would read him and Jessica too, and he delivered.

"You had a friend that died tragically," said John

"Yes," said Jay.

"He was shot. There was water," John Edward told him.

"Yes," said Jay. I could see that Jay was tearing up. His friend Danny died when he was growing up. John Edward gave him details of their relationship and told him that Danny was happy, that Danny says hello.

Next, John read my co-worker. Then he told us all to stick together because something was going to happen in March and we would all need each other's support. March 2020, the world shut down because of the pandemic. John Edward was right.

I learned that my life was more than just my DNA discovery that night. I had a colorful life. You might say that this was just another unusual event, or perhaps it is the icing on the cake. It depends on how you perceive what happened. Life is multi-dimensional.

Blair Robertson again

Blair has healing circles, which comprise ten people. You can book one of these sessions which were all online during the pandemic. You are guaranteed a reading. I was ready to talk with my bio father Frank this time. I wasn't fully ready with John Edward. But I was ready now. I was over two years into my discovery and we were stuck home because of the pandemic. I was bored.

We all met online. Blair took his usual potshots at therapists (psychic mediums are human, so they have to bring themselves in there) but I could get past that. I also made sure I told him how I felt about it before we all disconnected from the session.

"I see a father figure coming through," he says. "He is showing me he had a heart attack, but it was not because of heart disease." This means I am up. My father, Frank, died just a few days before his fifty-sixth birthday. He had kidney cancer and had survived. Rebecca told me that the heart attack was probably from all the chemo he had endured because of his kidney cancer coupled with the amount of alcohol he consumed.

It was my biological father coming through. Blair told me that my father knew about me. Father said that my parents did a good job raising me. Blair said, "The decision was in your best interest. He knew about you, as did the man who raised you." I could ask questions. "Was he the man in the mall who came to visit me when I was in college?" "Yes," Blair answered quickly and then continued, "He was curious how you turned out since he had not seen you in some time. There were more visits to see you that you were unaware of."

A year after this online session with Blair, I connected with one of my biological father's girlfriends who confirmed (because she keeps a journal and could verify information from years ago) that Frank announced to her one day in between Thanksgiving and Christmas in 1982, "I am going to see my daughter. She wants nothing to do with me. I have not seen her since she was a baby. I hope she will talk to me." You will read more about this later.

Brian Weiss, MD & Past Life Regressions

After getting my certification in hypnotherapy, I tried some past life regressions for myself. After several automatic regressions of some of my clients in my office, I wanted to have another experience and was reading Brian Weiss books. Dr. Weiss had a video that I worked through, and I had regressed to the day I was born. "Everyone is so happy," he said. "A new baby is born." He led us into our birth setting and described the elated emotions that the mother was feeling having this baby, and that's when a huge amount of dissonance hit me like a steamroller. In my own experience, my mother was extremely depressed when I finally said hello to the world for the first time. I did not understand it. It also gave me validation that a trained therapist should do hypnotherapy to help someone process the disturbing feelings that emerged during my birth. I suddenly was struck because my mother was depressed. I did not stand a chance with someone who was so sad because I entered an earthly existence.

Fast forward over ten years from that first event with Brian Weiss, MD, a well-known psychiatrist. I am now practicing hypnotherapy in my practice and had already had birth events on the scarlet couch in my office. I had a few past life regressions appear in those sessions (or a dream state, depending on the individual's belief system). By this time, I was into my ancestry discovery for a year plus. I was driving to the Omega Institute in Rhinebeck, NY when, suddenly, I had a profound epiphany. My mother was depressed when I was born because the man in the waiting room was not my biological father. My mother had a baby which ushered her in to purgatory.

I cannot fathom what she was feeling as my experience with the birth of each of my children was euphoric. After one of our sessions with Dr. Weiss, suddenly it felt like my entire birthing process came together. My mother was not depressed about me, personally. She was just dejected as the birth, no matter who popped out, was a consequence of her actions. I felt a tremendous sense of liberation. I was not the cause of my mother's sorrow. She was.

During that week, our group had regressed several times. Ironically enough, during one of those sessions, my daughter and I said goodbye and were sent to separate gas chambers to die.

It was powerful, as I could see the skeletons in piles below me as I drifted away towards the sky, apparently witnessing my death. When I awoke from that session, I realized I sat up straight and clobbered the person sitting next to me. I suppose I was Jewish in a past life, too.

8

LIFE IN SYNC

"In every moment, the universe is whispering to you. You're constantly surrounded by signs, coincidences, and synchronicities, all aimed at propelling you in the direction of your destiny."
—Denise Linn

"Hello, Alexandra," said Marvin, the Jewish insurance agent Alexandra used for years. He was a chubby, endearing man with light eyes and dark hair, and a sexy voice. If Alexandra had never met him in person, she would have fantasized he was an Adonis of sorts. He was a cantor in a local temple.

"Hi Marvin," Alexandra said. Marvin caught her in the middle of exploring her results on 23andMe, the second set of DNA tests Alexandra took that year. "Did you ever have your DNA tested?" Alexandra asked randomly.

"No," Marvin answered suspiciously. He probably worried he had some unknown child somewhere himself or that it was a government conspiracy or maybe he was the convicted felon the FBI was looking for. "What makes you ask that?"

"Are you sitting down?" Alexandra asks.

"Yes," was Marvin getting impatient? Alexandra couldn't tell because she was such a mess herself. These days, it was

hard to care when paranoia kicked in.

"I am Jewish," whispered Alexandra as though she were hiding in a basement from the gestapo.

There was silence on the other end of the phone.

"What are you talking about?" asked Marvin in a you-sound-ridiculous tone of voice.

"I took a DNA test. My dad is not my dad. My mother had an affair, and I am Jewish and Italian," Alexandra said, blurting out her newfound truth. Alexandra continued with a rush of emotion and jumbled words. She wouldn't tell Marvin how much she weighed for her insurance policy, but she was telling him this deep, dark secret.

"Wonderful!" Marvin sounded elated. "You are a landsman."

"Do you know what a landsman means?" asked Marvin.

"Yes," Alexandra replied. "It means compatriot. That was also my married name for eighteen years with the wasband."

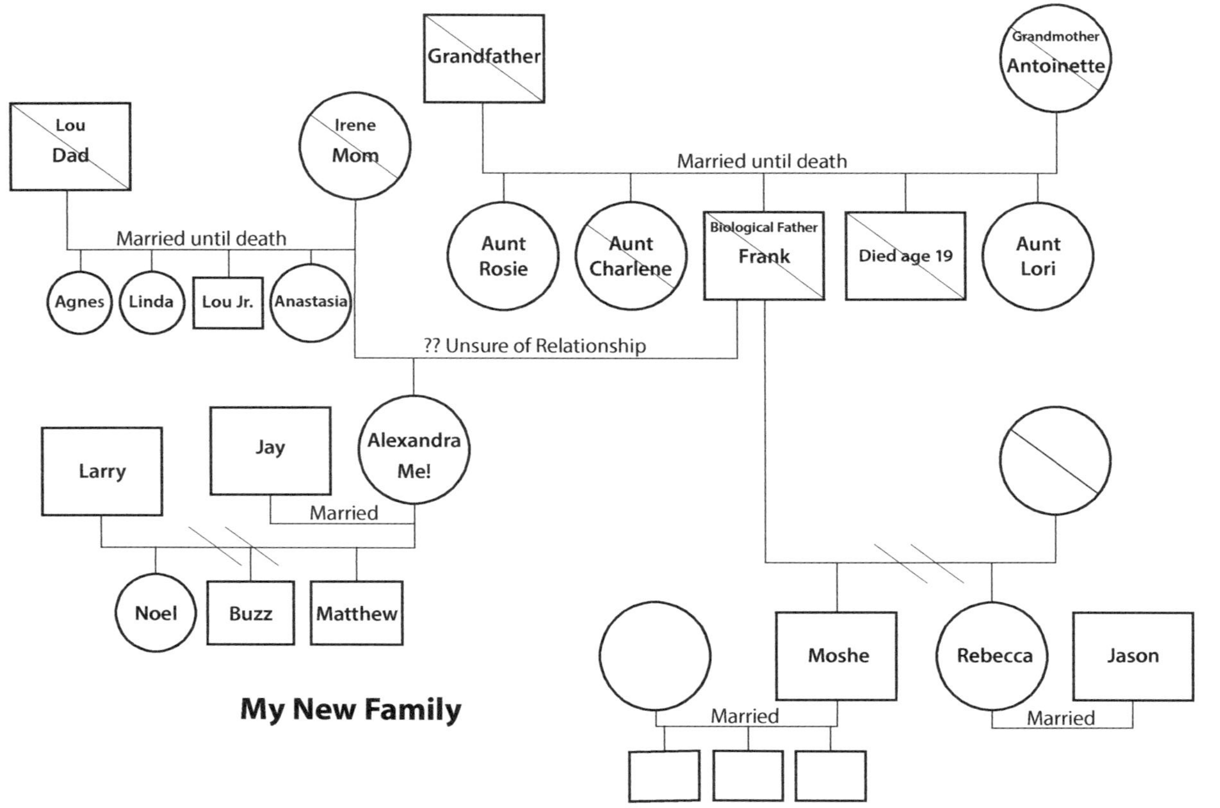

Lou
Dad
Irene
Mom
Grandfather
Grandmother
Antoinette
Married until death
Aunt Rosie
Aunt Charlene
Biological Father
Frank
Died age 19
Aunt Lori
Agnes
Linda
Lou Jr.
Anastasia
Married until death
?? Unsure of Relationship
Larry
Jay
Alexandra
Me!
Married
Noel
Buzz
Matthew
My New Family
Moshe
Rebecca
Jason
Married
Married

I believe we are all where we are supposed to be at a particular time for a reason. At the precise time I seem to need validation, a poignant memory seeps out of my subconscious, flowing freely to give me the answers I seek. I have had several strange coincidences and synchronicities during my life that seem now to be connected. When I was working with my mother in Ridgewood, NJ, I was filing travel brochures. One of my co-workers handed me a stack of Trade Wind Tours to Israel and Egypt and said, "Look at the cover. Who does that look like?" I peered at the picture and could not believe my eyes. It was me. Of course, it was not me, but I swore it was. There was this young, thin, curly haired, olive skin, green-eyed girl in a sexy, wispy white outfit posed on some ancient pillar staring back at me. It was uncanny. My mother was sitting at her desk, and I made her look at the brochure too. She couldn't believe what she was seeing either. Before you knew it, we caused a minor disturbance in the middle of a boring afternoon. I still have that brochure dated 1984. My mother saved a copy. I saved my copy. I found both brochure covers. Interesting, isn't it? I wonder if she ever shared the brochure with my biological father.

When I worked with my mother in Ridgewood, the office was across the street from Sealfons department store. Apparently, my biological grandmother shopped there frequently. So did my Aunt Rosie and sometimes my Aunt Charlene. Aunt Rosie and I talked about The Daily Treat, a diner with great food and a bright atmosphere. We both had lunch there on many occasions, just not with each other. My grandmother was with her sometimes. I wonder if we were ever there at the same time.

I was in college and dated two Ethans, one David, and one George. All these college men were Jewish. I met David's family in Howard Beach, NY, where there is a large Jewish population. My roommates habitually dragged me to Hillel dances because, "Alexandra, you attract Jewish men. We need you." I had long, dark, curly hair. I fell in love with Ethan, the prospective lawyer, my junior year of college. He used to show up at my dormitory unexpectedly for hugs, and happenstance would connect us on the main campus for college parties. We would meet at the pub, go to the library to study together, and had long conversations about what sex was like. I believe we were closeted virgins together.

Ethan was a year ahead of me and aspired to start law school the following fall. When he was ready to graduate, I purchased a huge balloon bouquet with all kinds of lawyer tchotchkes connected to the bottom of the balloons with a huge red bow. I was ready to take the plunge and tell Ethan how I felt about him. I thought we would spend the summer together since I was staying in New Brunswick, NJ at my job. Ethan loved his gift and then dropped the "You're not Jewish and I will never introduce you to my parents" bomb. I was devastated. I thought of reaching out to him to let him know forty years later so I could flaunt my new discovery and tell him I was not a shiksa. I am not sure what the desired outcome would be. I swore off all Jewish boyfriends after Ethan.

I had another dear friend who I never dated, but he was a Sephardic Jewish man who later became a doctor. He gave me Jewish advice when grandma was pissed at me because I gave my son his father's name as his middle name. Ashkenazi Jews name their babies after dead people and Sephardic Jews name their babies after living people they would like their child to emulate, is what David told me. He was my partner at a Rutgers University Dance-a-Thon for a charity. We had a blast. We never dated or crossed that boundary, although we talked about joining the Peace Corps together when we graduated.

I met my first husband, Larry, when I was a senior in college. I was living with three Jewish roommates who introduced me to Jewish culture. We had hallah bread every Friday and made French toast. I turned the lights on and off on Friday evenings into Saturday for my Orthodox roommate. The other two kept me updated on Jewish tradition as I asked a lot of questions. My roommates went home for the Jewish holidays which I loved because I had the apartment to myself. I pumped everyone for information on a quest to understand Judaism. I do not know why, but I was hungry for knowledge. I studied world religions and loved learning their impact on culture, and I was delighted to share my knowledge with Larry's parents when I first met them. I found out after the first date that despite the promise I made to avoid all Jewish men, no matter how charming, that Larry was a Jew and there was nothing I could do about it; it was happening anyway.

Sometimes we attract like members of society. To me, it feels like the Law of Attraction, like attracts like. Three out of four of my college roommates were Jewish. One of my best friends was and is Jewish. Larry wanted to cover up the cross in the church where we got married in order to avoid insulting the six Jewish relatives who bothered to come to our ceremony. There was no way I was asking a priest to cover up the icon of his religion and church. I married Larry in my church with the crucifix watching over us. We hired a rabbi from Brooklyn, and Larry broke the glass under his foot. Asking to cover up the cross for the relatives who took exception to the statue in the church I grew up in, felt like it was some kind of reverse discrimination. Why wasn't I ever good enough? Because I wasn't Jewish? I am now. My mother always told me I would marry a Jewish man. Obviously, she knew something I didn't know. My mother was spiritual, she bought in to the Law of Attraction.

Preceding Larry, I was always the shiksa, and I internalized the meaning that I was a non-Jew and undeserving of the circumcised. I was wrong, and for once, I am happy to admit this. I sang my shiksa title like a canticle in the woods, sung by a beauty with a ring of flowers in her hair wearing a funky white dress. All these years later, my daughter jokes with me and calls me "fellow Jew."

After Larry and I went our separate ways, I dated a loud, boisterous German man from a town near Heidelberg, Germany. Franz liked to accompany me to community outreach work events for a hospital I worked at because they were usually fun and never dull. Franz and I went to an outreach event at a scenic park in Lakewood, NJ, the home of a very large Hasidic population. I dressed in a long skirt, a long-sleeved blouse, and a hat to cover my head. I wanted to respect the Jewish folks who felt anything but respected in Lakewood because of political turbulence. I instructed Franz not to speak, as he had a very thick German accent. We made butterflies from coffee filters and clothespins all afternoon with children in the park. He said very little to the kids who came to the table to try their hand at our tie-dyed butterflies. One of the little ones sneezed. Franz said, "Gesundheit" and I was mortified. Of course, there really wasn't any reason to be mortified, I realize now. I didn't then.

Franz and I talked about what it was like to grow up in Germany and he informed me that where he went to school, the history of World War II included little about Adolf Hitler. It always hurt his feelings if someone called him a Nazi. I wonder how he would feel now, knowing he was dating a Jewish woman. Franz was an entrepreneur who flew back and forth between the United States and Paris. Though financially, I would have been set if we ended up together, I could not stand the unwarranted pot shots he would take at me, not to mention he had some commitment phobia. Ol' Franz hated his mother. I should have known.

I met Jay via a computer dating site. The first thing I asked him was what his relationship was like with his mother. Being a therapist, I could get away with that line of questioning. After the wasband, who hated his mother, and then the boyfriend that hated his mother, I was not taking any chances. We have been together for almost twenty years. When I first discovered my heritage, Jay and I talked about Hanukkah and that this was my very first quasi-celebrating as a Jewish person. I told Jay I needed a bib for my first Hanukkah. We lit our battery-operated menorah the first night and listened to Adam Sandler sing his holiday song. Since nobody spoke any Hebrew, we did not know how to sing any songs after lighting the first candle. To my surprise, Jay handed me a small box wrapped in blue paper. You guessed it, my bib with the words, "My first Hanukkah, 2018." He took a picture of me, and we laughed for hours after that. I had a horrible cold. I had a lot of ailments that first year. My mother used to say that colds were emotional. She was correct. Fast forward two years and I don't know what possessed me to ask Jay, but I made him fork over his DNA test so I could inspect it. We always called him the Italian wannabee. He was now calling me the Swedish wannabee. As luck would have it, Jay turned out to be one percent Jewish. I bought him a "Baby's First Hanukkah" bib that year.

My new "little" brother, Moshe, and my nephew, Agnes' son, have the same first name. My nephew is a little over two years younger than I am. He tells everyone, "We were raised like siblings. Alexandra is more like a big sister to me." He wasn't wrong. Remember, his mother Agnes had the "second mother" title. I took him to many of his firsts, including his first Billy Joel concert. Buzz tells me he shares a lot of firsts he had with me when they are together. It makes Buzz smile and it makes me happy that he remembers. Both my brother and my nephew, who share the same first name, are involved in law enforcement. My nephew is a vehicular traffic accident investigator. My brother is an ambulance chaser who represents individuals in traffic accidents. They both grew up in the same town. My brother is the same age as my niece and they were in the same class in the same high school.

When I visited Rebecca in her apartment in Rutherford, the first thing I noticed was the clock in the kitchen. It was a chef with a clock where his belly would be. I had my kitchen decorated with chefs. I had the same clock in my kitchen. Rebecca has a shihtzu. All of my original sisters had shihtzus. All my sisters have or had shihtzus.

My dad vs. biological father's health history is not all that different except my bio father died at a very young age. They were both "funny" and "witty." They were both the family chef. Initially, I wondered why my mom would cheat on my dad with someone who was so much like him from what I initially heard. Of course, paradoxically, I am glad my mother did have that one indiscretion that I know of. When I was researching my biological father because Moshe holds his pictures and his history hostage, I learned that my biological father dressed up like Santa Claus for some political event. He was rather cute in his Santa suit, which was a parody of the state of politics in his town. I made a collage on one of my apps that put my dad and my father next to each other, both dressed like Santa Claus for different reasons. I am puzzled where Frank got his idea from, but I also know that my mom sewed my dad's Santa suit. Did she let him borrow that Santa suit? My mom used to lend it to anyone who asked.

My mother gave me bits and pieces of information growing up. I have a pretty little pink dress that I wore in first grade. I wore it for Easter with an adorable bonnet and I have a picture of me in that dress. "Mr. and Mrs. B(Italian last name) sent that dress for you." Why would Mr. and Mrs. Italian last name that started with a B send that dress for me when they did not know me? Maybe that was my biological father at work again?

There was another memory that came into my consciousness just after my discovery. I was in my twenties, working at a travel agency in the mall. I was decorating for Christmas with dolls my mom purchased for me from all around the world. It was my first time decorating a window with no one telling me what I should do. The owner gave me carte blanche which I loved because I had such creative ideas.

There were tufts of cottony snow and a swing suspended from the ceiling. I placed dolls from all over the world intending to entice people to come on in and book their dream travel excursions with the promise of wrapping gift certificates with shiny bows. I was Santa's elf, after all, and I knew how to wrap gifts. While I was placing snow and standing in the window wearing a green striped dress my mother bought me, I heard the owner and his mother whispering behind me at the desk just past mine. They were intently watching a man who was peering in the window. He was staring directly at me. As creepy as it could appear, I was not worried. I kept on decorating. This mysterious man was in his mid to late forties, had thinning hair, compassionate eyes, and was wearing a dark overcoat, either dark gray or black, and he had his hands in his pockets.

I continued to don the window in Christmas cheer and watched out of the corner of my eye. The owner of the business and his mom were panicking. I wasn't clear if they were worried that I would be accosted and there was some additional speculation that the man owned a travel agency in the next town and would try to recruit me. They weren't completely wrong. My biological father owned an insurance and real estate company, but it was in Monmouth County. We were in Middlesex. I finally had enough of the whispering. Besides, there was too much commotion with holiday shoppers in the mall and I couldn't hear what they were saying behind my back. I jumped out of the window and weeded my way through the bustling shopping crowds to the gazing stranger.

"Do you like it?" I asked.

Oddly enough, the man never looked me in the face, never gazed into my eyes. I was wondering if this enigmatic stranger with the slight grin was attracted to me or something, and I was puzzled and curious.

"I like everything you do," he answered in a soft voice.

That was it. There were no other interactions that I could recall. This tall, dark, and handsome stranger in an overcoat was elusive. What is interesting to me is that this memory never crossed my mind before, not until I found out my dad was not my biological father.

Rebecca told me that sounds like something our father would say. Aunt Charlene told me that my father did not wear overcoats. Of course, I have a picture of him wearing an overcoat.

When I graduated from Douglass, though initially bragging to anyone who would listen about his last of five children as the first college graduate in the family, my dad Lou became despondent and distant. He was panicked and insisted we drive the hour home and skip the planned celebrated lunch after the long ceremony. My dad's behavior was uncharacteristically upset, considering the joyous occasion. I wonder now if my father Frank was somewhere lurking in the crowd and if my mother disclosed to my dad Lou that she told Frank I was graduating college.

I was attending a writer's workshop up in Rhinebeck, NY. From there, I was going to visit my new family for a few days. I decided, as I was writing my feelings about my DNA discovery since it was a memoir workshop, that I would visit the gravesites of my biological father, my uncle, and my grandparents, none of whom I ever met that I know of.

While I was in NY, I purchased clear acrylic stones with tiny, delicate white angels in the middle. I had several well-meaning co-workshop attendees tell me that Jews do not believe in angels. During my time in Rhinebeck, I had a plethora of well-meaning individuals, mostly writers, giving me advice on "how" to be Jewish. I purchased four angel stones. I had never been to a Jewish cemetery in my life. I bought three angels and one archangel since angels have a hierarchy and my father was going to be the recipient of the archangel. I would like to think it was Archangel Michael since I went to St. Michael's School from kindergarten through eighth grade.

While I was in the parking lot, the workshop facilitator, Nancy Aronie, was waiting for her ride back to Massachusetts. Nancy reminds me of Jane Fonda's character in "Grace and Frankie". Nancy helped me to put words on the paper and Nancy helped me to lose the fear I was harboring in writing a memoir. I stopped to talk with her briefly while she was a captive audience. Nancy, I asked on a whim, "Can I leave a stone at a Jewish cemetery with an angel in it? Someone in our workshop told me that Jews don't believe in angels."

"Of course you can," Nancy answered quickly. "I believe in angels."

"Well, I never went to a Jewish cemetery before. That is what my memoir is about," I told her and then continued, "I did not know I was Jewish until a few years ago."

"I knew it! You are a landsman," Nancy announced.

Wow. So, I had two people who told me I was a landsman plus I had that name for almost twenty years. I try not to step on anyone's cultural toes, but that seemed to seal my fate. I wondered for just a moment if it would have been fun to keep the last name. I left the workshop/retreat and drove the three hours to my next destination, determined to find some closure. I was on my way to the Jewish cemetery in Saddlebrook, NJ with a map in hand to visit my new family's plot. My Aunt Charlene tended those graves for years. I had seen pictures of my father's grave, but I was never inclined or ready to venture there. I was on a mission which I had hoped would lead me to closure.

I figured after three plus years, it was time. I did not know what I would be doing. My arrival at the cemetery was exactly at 3:27pm. Three twenty-seven is also my birthday. Perhaps that was a hello from heaven. Maybe it was an omen that I was exactly where I was supposed to be now and always. I drove to the section where the graves were located. I parked my rental car, took out my towel to rest on, and hoped that I wasn't parked on anyone's grave.

I had my face buried in a cemetery map. It was like looking at a foreign language. First, I was trying to match gravestones to paper with eyes that do not see all that well. I gazed quizzically at Hebrew, stars of David, gardens named after ancient prophets and full family plots of people that nobody visits. I felt like dropping a stone off at every grave so that the departed knew I was there and was saying hello. I care about you, even though you died in 1947.

I stared at the page and gazing up; I knew I was in the right vicinity. It was eerily quiet, with a slight breeze rustling the remaining dried autumn leaves in occasional swirls. I might as well have been standing in a rice field somewhere in Southeast Asia because it felt like I was in a foreign country. As I stared at the map and rotated the page to fit the description on the avenue I walked along, I looked up and there before me I saw the most beautiful doe I had ever seen. This doe stood behind the family plot guiding my direction. This memory played its reel in black and white with shades of gray, but my heart bled crimson. She was twenty feet away from me. Deer foster serenity in my soul. If I am upset or angry or name the emotion de jour, when I see a deer, I forget what I am feeling and a deer brings me back to the present and places me instantaneously in a state of suspended animation. I thought it was rather touching that the universe or God or whatever you want to call that supreme being who has my back twenty-four seven said, "Alexandra, you need a deer to bring you peace." Tears of anticipation and complicated grief began to flow and I felt for a moment I had transcended to another plane. That moment in time was beyond my comprehension and usually something that only happens in movies. But the fact of the matter is, this happened to me at the perfect time, the perfect day, with the perfect weather to visit my father for the first time, even though he was buried six feet beneath the ground. They called for rain that day, but it was one of the most beautiful days we had that week. Ironically enough, the deer was standing right next to the Barrie family grave site.

First, I spent time with my paternal grandmother, Antoinette Barrie. I am Antoinette Barrie's oldest granddaughter whom she never knew, whom she couldn't claim. From everything I heard about her, things would have been different if Grandma Antoinette had a choice. There was something about being in the presence of my previously unknown family, even if only spiritually, that felt right. There was a connection, a connection I needed to help me heal. I walked to each grave and touched the stone gently. There were rocks there from previous visitors. I am guessing Aunt Charlene left them.

My grandfather had a very high-powered union job. He and my grandmother had to move to Canada for his work. My young uncle was staying with his family in New Jersey. At nineteen, he died in a tragic car accident. He was in the car with a member of a famous rock band from the 60s and 70s. This was the accident my mother read about in the *Herald News*. My grandfather died young of a broken heart; my brother-in-law shared that my grandparents moved for "health reasons." This fed into my "I am a mob princess" daydream I entertained for about a month that Aunt Lori teased me about. My grandfather was Sicilian and converted from Roman Catholicism to Judaism to marry my grandmother.

I stood staring at Frank Barrie, "loving brother, loving father" before I spread out the towel I brought with me to sit on. I wept.

Sitting down, I talked to Frank. Thank God there was nobody around except for dead people and deer. "Hi Frank, it is me, Alexandra, your daughter. It was about time I came and sat on your lap." I giggle between teardrops, thinking how funny I am. I am at a loss for words but am not void of tears and corny jokes. "I thought I would sit here with you for a little while." I talked some more with my unknown dad, then cried until there were no tears left. Fortunately for me, I was in an older part of the cemetery, so I was alone in my grief and chatter.

Kissing a finger to each gravestone, I took my exit. I said goodbye and found there were more tears to cry as I exited. Promising my newfound family I would come back for a visit, I headed towards the car thinking that maybe next time it might be kind to bring more pebbles for my family's neighbors. "You are all not forgotten. Please don't forget about me. I love you, even though I don't know you." How strange is that?

That day, one of my wounds felt healed. I gave myself permission to care and to love these predecessors who were part of my blood. There was no hiding how I felt. After spending that time with my ancestors, it was less important to me what my mother's and biological father's relationship was. No more was it a long-term relationship or a fling or did my father get depressed because he had to give up his child and couldn't share that pain? It didn't matter if there was love besides lust between my biological parents. What happened under the sheets didn't seem to matter, even though it did not stay there. I gave up the idea of knowing every single, solitary, detailed fact about how I came to be. The fact was, I was meant to be. Here I am. I turned a major corner, at least in that instant, at least for the hour, at least for that day, and the latest epiphany was treasured in the moment. Cemeteries not only have the potential to bring peace, but they have the possibility to bring closure.

9

———

FORGIVENESS IS NOT THE "F" WORD

*"Most of us can forgive and forget; we just don't want the other person
to forget that we forgave."*
—Ivern Ball

Let's be honest, this was the hardest chapter of all to write because it's time to face some demons whenever you mention that "F" word. Don't hate me. We don't forgive for others, we don't let the others get away with anything, we forgive for ourselves so that we can move on in the business of living. It would be too easy to blame our parents, but our parents are humans after all. Hanging on to negative thoughts and feelings does nothing for you but cause you more pain. Forgiveness is the dreaded, elusive concept that sends people into a tailspin at the mere mention of the word.

Several years ago, I organized a retreat on forgiveness. Surprise, surprise, only one person signed up. One of the inherent problems people seem to possess stems from the idea that when we forgive, we are letting someone off the hook. Everyone thought forgiveness was a good idea, everyone bought into a retreat intending to walk away somehow screaming, "I'm healed!", but to decide to forgive was not in anyone's repertoire. I realized that if I want to do another retreat on forgiveness, I will have to call it something else.

Forgiveness, as a concept to even fathom comprehending, I tell my clients, is "seventy times seven." I am quoting the Jesus metaphor with the disclaimer that I am not a religious zealot attempting to convert anyone. This particular metaphor is easy to understand and helps make some sense of this elusive concept that makes some people cringe. Talking about the concept of forgiveness is no effortless task and people have told me over the years that they, too, struggle to let someone off the hook. Your capacity to forgive being related to your capacity to love is powerful, and the concept made me cry once. In reality, it felt like a lot of work. It felt like I was a bad person if I chose not to forgive. Connecting my capacity to forgive with my capacity to love did not seem quite right, either. It made me feel guilty if I felt like I was unforgiving. I guess I was brainwashed and this time, I refuse to go to confession.

Forgive and forget is another concept that feels both improbable and naïve. Most people are of the opinion that forgetfulness is part of the package. How would a person learn the life lessons attached to granting clemency if the crime was not remembered? My friend Pastor Joe told me that once you decide to forgive, you don't have to go back to being a doormat. We were talking about Linda, one of my originals. I told Pastor Joe how Linda and I walked along the boardwalk once in Pt. Pleasant, NJ heading towards the inlet, having a pleasant day just chatting about nothing. He asked me if I wanted to make a human tea bag out of her. I was validated by Pastor Joe, although I laughed so hard, I snorted. Pastor Joe knew what I was feeling, and he knew the task in front of me would not be easy. Pastor Joe only knew the half of it, as did I.

Like forgiveness, letting go is a conscious decision first, then a concerted effort to release the negative energy associated with an event or person(s) who cause us pain. It takes time, patience, and work. Like so much of this journey, it is a process. Whining, I say, "Why do I have to do all the work?" The answer is straightforward, but the mechanics are not. I was free every time I made a conscious decision to forgive and with each time I released or let go of the angst towards another, all four hundred and ninety times, I was one step closer to being myself again.

When I was a little girl, maybe eleven or twelve, my mother and I had a conversation about abortion. Without recalling all the details, I remember my mom became angry with me. My mother told me something I know she regretted for the rest of her life because she told me so. "Alexandra, I wish I had an abortion instead of having you." My mother apologized for that angry statement more times than can be remembered. Sometimes that apology came at the most inopportune times, usually after it was forgotten for a few years, only to remind me again. The pain in that statement reoccurred, only to be forgiven yet another time. It felt like I was being tested on some cosmic level. The child that I was at the time was wounded.

Forgiveness was essential, or I would never talk to my mother again. My mother's guilt was justified for saying something so awful, but I wish she did not keep sharing her guilt with me. It was time to apply the "seventy times seven" rule. I couldn't forget because my mom kept reminding me. My mother really needed to work on forgiving herself first. Self-forgiveness is the first task in deciding to forgive. This process is uncomfortable, but it is a necessary component of self-respect and loving yourself enough to set boundaries, enough to start a process that will eventually set you free to be perfectly you.

Step One: decide to forgive. That is the first step towards freedom.

During one of my therapy sessions, my therapist told me I was neglected as a child. I could not accept that because, as an adult, I did not feel that way until after my mother died. Then that old wound surfaced after her death. My mom was emotionally neglectful. My biological father was not present. As an adult, I can intellectualize, but as a small child, I was abandoned. My dad, the man who raised me, was the primary nurturer. I believe that was a conscious decision on his part. My adult self understands intellectually why my mother sometimes neglected my nurturing. The child that I was did not have the intellectual capacity to understand what was going on. Putting together the whole forgiveness package by allowing my inner child to express the feelings she stuffed inside for so long was cathartic. There is a reason for the adage, "the truth hurts." The cliché about the truth setting us free is not a total lie. It just takes time and patience to work through the truth, however traumatic that truth turns out to be.

Deciding to forgive is a process that takes time. When I mention forgiveness to my NPE clients, I have a sense they might quit therapy. Belief systems, anger, sadness, shame, guilt, grief, unreconciled trauma, believing that accountability needs to be assigned and perhaps compensated, a desire for retribution, are all part of the reconciliation process a person needs to chew on and digest when making the decision to forgive. It's scary to face the demons within. The decision should not be made in haste. It is deciding, "I would like to work on forgiveness." Make sure that before you decide to forgive, you allow yourself the time and space to feel every single feeling you have towards the individual you are working on forgiving. Don't deny yourself the anger or sadness or uncomfortable feelings you have. Give yourself the permission to wallow in it. Own those feelings. Locate the feelings in your body. Watch for repercussions such as stomach aches or digestive issues if you store your sadness in your stomach. Be mindful of feelings in your chest, for that is home to your heart. Allow your heart to speak, journal if you can. If your heart or stomach had a voice, what words of wisdom or feelings would they express? You might want to journal WIFM, or What's In It For Me? What would your life look like if you forgave that person who wronged you? Remember you are not expected to forget. It impedes your learning process. How would you feel if you were free from the feelings you are harboring? What roadblocks are standing in your way? Roadblocks may take the form of the unfinished business of processing complicated feelings.

Step Two: Forgive yourself. I had to do it in many areas of my life. I had to look at my own mistakes in my own life since I made so many. But were these events mistakes? Some of life's occasions have proven to be spiritual accidents. Every decision we make affects someone else in a ripple effect. Every individual we meet shares a connection with us over varying degrees of time. Prior to knowing each other, for example, my husband Jay and I were parked on opposite sides of a train track and we each witnessed the train crush the car of an elderly couple while they were still inside. We found that out a few years into our relationship. I was offered a job at the school where Jay's wife at the time worked, but I did not possess the school certification to accept the position. If I had taken that job, I never would have dated my husband. Instead, I got another job, then Jay and I met on a popular dating site a few months after his divorce was finalized.

I had to forgive myself for many events over the years before I could decide to forgive anyone else. Forgiveness would be a lengthy topic for another book. Sometimes, I had to admit that I was human. I had a work supervisor named Cliff who I would sometimes confess my shortcomings to, and he was kind enough to let me off the hook by saying, "You mean you are human?" I never forgot what Cliff said, and I have passed that information along to others. It is a necessary gift we can give ourselves, the right to be human, the right to make mistakes. Then, perhaps, we can get to self-forgiveness.

If you are an NPE, this might have many dimensions for you, depending on your original family situation. So many NPEs have birth certificate fathers who were not at all like my dad. It would be easy if self-forgiveness had steps to it and it was not so multi-dimensional. In my story, I had to forgive my original siblings again, perhaps to complete some unfinished business. It still hurts when I think about two of the five originals knowing something for several years and not sharing that information with me. I am working on that. I forgive myself for feeling stupid. I could not have known, although every picture I look at now screams of a child who does not fit in with the rest of the crew. I forgive myself for my part in our spoiled relationships. I forgive myself for feeling bad about wanting immediate answers. I forgive myself for the intense, anger at my mother, so much so in the beginning of this journey, that I could not even speak of her.

I forgive myself for sometimes impulsively blurting things out to people throughout this journey. In the world of reaction vs. response, it has taken years for me to learn to respond more and react less. I had to learn to forgive myself for my reactions. Yes, I am human with human emotions and feelings, and I have to learn the lesson like everyone else—to care for myself first.

Step Three: Forgive everyone else, one at a time. This included my mother, my dad, my biological father, my original siblings, and Moshe.

My dad predeceased my mom by eighteen months. I knew it would not be long after he died, since she seemed to spend most of her waking hours with him after she retired. My mother was cognizant enough to know of his death, but she did not speak a great deal. She booked me fake trips to Chicago when she was in her happy place because of her dementia. Every time I would leave her I whispered, "I forgive you." I was not sure what I was forgiving her for, but I did it every time I left her. I don't think she was aware of what I was saying. It was not important that she understood, as I spoke those three words for me. How prophetic.

My mom loved to write. In those days, it was more difficult since the typewriters were very large and very clunky and awkward. Thank heavens that the electric typewriter came into being and my mom was one of the first to have such a creation. She didn't need correct-o-type. When mom was sad, she would pound the keys. I found a box with some of my mom's journals and writings.

When my mom died, I read her own written words as a tribute at her funeral, sharing the wisdom she possessed in her own words. In retrospect, this bit of prose offered hints of how alone she was feeling right around the time I was growing up. She was in her forties. My mother was struggling with holding down a career, managing a family, and having a relationship with my dad, which did not feel emotionally fulfilling based on what she wrote.

My mother was writing about me. It is published here, unedited:

By: Irene Pederson, mom (written circa 1964)

"Mommy, let me put your earrings on the television." With this, the three-year-old skipped to the TV with earrings that felt so heavy after a full day.

"Come, sit on my lap," said the mother of this fast-growing child, loved so much, but denied so much of her mother's personal attention during the day.

"Why, did you miss me?"

"Oh yes, so very much. Now you be a good girl so that pretty soon mommy can stay with you all the time. Did you have fun today?"

"Oh yes, mommy, we played school, and Christmas, and… now wait here, mommy, I'll be right back. I want to go to my daddy."

She sprung from her mother's lap and jumped on to daddy's.

Mixed emotions, packed moments of affection, and discipline rushed into a few minutes in the evening, as well as the early morning, when little one is dressed in a sweater over her pajamas to "taxi" her big sister, to work, and then home for breakfast and preparations for the day.

"Where am I going today, mom?" "Who is staying with me today?" "Why can't you stay home with me? Tiny's mother is home every day." "Don't you love me?" "Can I wear my

bride dress today with my veil and flowers and go get my prince?" "Please mommy, why don't you answer me?"

The thoughts have to be fast, many, and the words in short sentences. There is always so little time to go into the details. So much is important, but mother doesn't seem to think so. She is always so busy doing chores and telling her little one to "wait a minute." To a small child of three, whose associations in life with older brothers and sisters, strangers, friendly but lonely people, imagination runs away with her. With the help of books, TV, and her ever continuous questions her mentality increases to such an extent that no adult believes her age. Thus, more is expected of her by her family and only her daddy and mommy can give her the sense of security of being loved and understood.

The world is filled with such emotions in this day of progressive and better living, demanding so much more of the wife, housekeeper, and mother. In order to keep up with the times (not always the Jones family) but like the jet in transportation, the present generation's speed and way of life wants and demands deluxe, never satisfied with first class, and if in the second-class category, then yells for first class, a mother realizes that this is our way of life today. To refuse it is to be unhappy, lonely, and live a distressed existence.

A mother of today (usually brought up in a large family and taught to help, to make the most of every situation) will experience deep pangs of hunger for the life of a cherished female of the "good old days" when women did not have to compete with men. These pangs grown on a weary day when the vitamins don't help, or the story you watch after a long day is a bit emotional, or someone forgot to smile or say, "hi." It is like the stroke of a cat's back the wrong way.

In the course of a full life with many friends and acquaintances, you will come upon these working wives and mothers. Their husbands and fathers of their children are a happy, *carefree lot, really enjoying their lives, and should you be inquisitive in a personal friendly way, you would soon find out that these wonderful husbands and fathers excuse themselves at times from the Golden Rule set forth by our heritages, feeling they deserve some fun in life. These working wives are so little fun, always busy, little time for laughter, just worry, so needlessly, they think. This could work two ways, but the important thing is that we are getting away from the wonderful, blissful life so enjoyed in courtship and the first years of marriage.*

This should not be. A word to you, mothers and working wives, "Today is yesterday's tomorrow." Keep that love light burning and make it the important part of your life. The many details we worry so about will all straighten out and, like a grain of sand on a wide beach, will prove so trivial. We'll be glad we didn't get so concerned. And to you men and fathers, take heed. Don't force women to compete with you. They don't really want to…it is only an "out" of mixed emotions working for the ones you love.

My mom sounded so alone in her struggles. In context, her writing feels like she was working on her own absolution. In later years, my mom had few close friends, and she spent most of her free time tending to her grandchildren, whom she loved. Somehow, I related to her loneliness as an adult, as it was part of my own experience. It was a connection we shared.

When my mother died, our relationship was better than okay. My mom and I had a long time loving and friendly relationship with each other. God, how I miss having coffee with her every morning. Mom suffered towards the end with Parkinson's and then Lewy Body dementia. I was her biggest advocate. I was with her the day she was diagnosed. It was a tender moment I will never forget. She said, "I'll beat this." I took her from the neurologist's office to the beach, where we sat on a bench so that she could have some time to process the sentence she was just handed. Both my mom and dad lived with my growing family for four years before I had to pass the baton to Agnes, due to chaotic sibling struggles that created challenges for me and my family. I was a sandwich generationer which means I was caring for elderly parents and very young children. We had a multi-generational household. It was great for the first three years, but it was sometimes like pulling teeth to get additional support from my siblings. Even with help in the home, my beeper, which I wore at my waist, was constantly going off with toilets overflowing, falls, and toaster fires. Denial of our parents' declining health led to powerful arguments with my originals. I was constantly dealing with a plethora of armchair quarterbacks attempting to dictate my family's life and what felt like constant judgment. Caregiving struggles were part of the package, yet I would not trade those years we had spent together as a multi-generational family.

Although my mother and I had that wonderful relationship for so long, after mom died I struggled with reconciling our relationship from my childhood. The lack of connection caused me a great deal of pain. It bothered me because I did not understand it and I was haunted because I could not shake whatever this unnamed feeling was that I harbored. When we all lived together with my parents, I papered over my childhood wounds to care for them. Once my parents were gone, the wounds which were not processed were ripped open. Ruminating on childhood, I was having such a hard time letting go. It made little sense. When this DNA discovery happened, I felt relief mixed in with my grief and other emotions. I allowed myself to feel bitter and angry because I knew it was a necessary part of my healing process. Knowing I did not cause my mother's pain was liberating. But I first had to go through the infuriated, raging resentment going on internally in order to get to liberation. I have stopped pining my mother-child relationship woes; those feelings have completely vanished. I must have hit my four hundred and ninetieth number of the forgiveness quota. It was clear by the end of my dad's life, my parents had worked out their differences. If dad could forgive my mom, there was no reason for me to bear the burden staying angry for too long.

My dad, Lou, modeled forgiveness and unconditional love. He taught me a lot. I learned that blood and DNA doesn't matter and that in every sense of the word, he was my father. I wrote songs and poetry about him as a teenager. He was my hero. He retired when I started college. I collected some of his Social Security because he was retired. It helped pay for my college education and he made up for any financial differences. I worked while I was in college.

The only question I had and still revisit is why my dad didn't tell me. I believe he knew because of my resemblance to my biological father. When my father was close to dying, he requested I take my kids to see their paternal grandparents (long story short, the wasband had a tenuous relationship with his parents, which meant no grandparent visits). Taking my children to see their grandparents was one of the first tasks on my list of things to do after my dad died. Going on the supposition that my dad knew of our mutual lack of shared biology, early on, I couldn't understand how someone who was so adamant about me making that connection for my children would not share his knowledge of my biological heritage. I had a paternal grandmother who was still alive at the time. I was mulling this over with my dear friend and Jeannie told me that she thought my father was afraid of losing me so close to the end of his own life. I forgive him if that was the reason. I feel closer to him in some respects as we were both innocents who somehow forged a connection that I carry with me every day of my life.

Agnes and Anastasia still need forgiveness. That is a work in progress. I forgive them for some of their nonsense of the past. However, I am diligently working on processing my forgiveness that they were keeping my ancestry secret. What I have found is that when someone lies, if they keep telling the same story over and over again, they eventually believe their own lies. Agnes back peddled when she was confronted about hiding the truth. I believe I would have had a lot more respect for her if she were just honest. Now, I own trust issues. The first people you trust unconditionally are your parents. You must do this as you rely on them for survival. Once that trust is violated, it becomes a constant challenge to trust anyone. The primary relationships seem to need healing first. Healing comes through the process of forgiveness.

Step Four: Forgive again the next time the same person or situation hurts you. The event is in the past and you have already forgiven, and yet you will be reminded of that other's transgressions from time to time. Forgive again and remember, it takes a while to get to seventy times seven. Metaphorically, you will need to forgive and let go at least four hundred and ninety times until the event or person loses complete power.

Step Five: Congratulate yourself. In the unending process it takes to achieve forgiveness, acknowledge your hard work. Pat yourself on the back, you deserve it. Forgiveness is something you will have to struggle with for most of your life. Someone will tell you to forgive, and you may tell them to go to hell, but remember, we forgive for ourselves and not the other person. People do not forgive because they perceive forgiveness as weakness. The inverse is true. Forgiveness is not for the faint of heart or the weak and weary.

So, forgiveness is the f word. It is about (f)reedom, (f)earlessness, and a (f)ruitful, (f)antastic life. I know the concept is difficult, but if forgiveness was easy, there would be no need for therapy, and I would be out of a job.

10

HIRAETH

"I had spent my whole life feeling homesick. The only difference between the two of us was that I didn't know what or where home was."

—unknown

When I learned of my NPE status, I had heard the term "hiraeth" from several sources in the support groups I became involved in. The term hiraeth, a Welsh word, simply put, is a feeling of homesickness for a place someone has never been. Though difficult to explain since it is defined as a feeling, hiraeth is a word that most NPEs and adoptees (even those with open adoptions) understand and relate to. In my work, I have shared this word with several of my clients who smile and relate to the concept. One benefit of having my discovery, however traumatizing it was in the beginning, is that the experience has made me a better and more compassionate therapist who understands on a profound level what it feels like to experience hiraeth. Coming to this conclusion took me a few years. Putting aside all denial, it was necessary to feel and express the anger and sadness and confusion in order to make sense of the situation.

Experiencing coming home was both new and familiar to me.

The newness had to do with my new family, while some of this journey also had to do with finding out that I was home already. It is just that a few new rooms were added to my home. For years, I had a recurring dream of walking through a large house. This house was my home, but there were rooms I did not have access to. Some doors were locked, and I did not possess a key. There was one room I could see into that felt like the recesses of a castle you might see in an old Dracula movie, complete with giant spider webs. The only visible colors playing on the grainy silver screen were black and white, with shades of gray. You could smell the dust and dinginess. I had always thought it had something to do with our home at the shore, which was a mother-daughter house with 3000 square feet. Perhaps I was returning to a nightmare of sorts. There were too many rooms to keep track of and too many demands sapping my energy like juggling growing children, sibling battles and ailing parents. I thought that recurring dream had to do with settling some deep part of my subconscious mind and all the unexplored neurons that were not connecting.

These rooms only appeared in my sleep. I just didn't care. It was not a nightmare; it was a recurring dream. Like many dreams, it never made sense, and I couldn't figure out what my subconscious was trying to accomplish. Then the DNA discovery occurred, and I had one last dream I could remember before the dream stopped completely. I was walking through this same home I had been to so many other times before. This time, one of the larger rooms had a different door. It was a garage door. I reached from the bottom instinctually presuming it would not be locked and I flung the door open.

The brightly lit room had two large windows and a little boy with shiny, curly hair was kneeling on a chair, eating something yummy at the table. He was sitting in front of one of the large open windows where white linen curtains were gently blowing in the breeze. The color of the room was in stark contrast to the dinginess I had visited so many times before. It was the same room, but this time, the energy in the space was transformed. Outside, I could see the green grass and the clothesline with sheets blowing gently back and forth. The room was full of warm light. There were children playing and laughing out in the back yard. I looked at pictures of people I did not know hanging on the wall in between the two windows. My intuition told me these people were deceased. Perhaps they were the same people I visited in the Jewish cemetery that I never met. It felt blissful compared to the rest of the house. It was like Dorothy opening the door from her black and white world into Oz, just before she meets Glinda, the good witch.

The dream was confirmation of my awakening. It was moving from cobwebs and staleness to fresh linen curtains and sheets (one of my favorite things growing up was sleeping on sheets that were clothesline dried). I never dreamed of that house where my access was limited again. If I can do hypnosis on my child learning to discover prebirth memory, then it would make sense that on a cellular level, I had always known that something was missing and even my subconscious mind was searching to find what was behind closed doors.

Meeting Rebecca, my new sister, for the first time had that "I'm home" feeling, although I was traumatized and sleep deprived. Meeting Aunt Charlene, Aunt Lori, Aunt Samantha, and Aunt Rosie all had that same feeling of connection and belonging. Aunt Rosie told me once that I provided a brand-new dimension to her life. That's profound for a ninety-year-old woman to say. Although she told me initially she wanted nothing to do with me, which I have never let her hear the end of and we laugh about now, I knew I had found a kindred spirit. Both Aunt Rosie and Aunt Lori gave me something that had come from my grandmother as a keepsake. Aunt Lori gave me a ring with the initial "A" on it, and of course the amethyst ring from my father. Aunt Rosie gave me a brass tray from my grandmother's collection. I wear the ring sometimes and the tray has a prominent place in my china cabinet.

Rebecca gave me any pictures she could find of our father. I couldn't meet these deceased family members, but I do have tangible souvenirs now. I have the picture of Aunt Charlene at her Kitchen Aid framed in gold and hanging in my kitchen, memorializing her and celebrating a perfect day. I feel connected now, something I hadn't felt since my dad, Lou, died. Rebecca, her husband, and my aunts have all been the reason for this. I have never felt so connected to a family and so disconnected from my original family. The disconnection has provided the space that allows me to move forward on the forgiveness train.

Other NPEs report similar experiences of living in alternate realities. One Saturday afternoon, I called Rebecca on my way to deliver a pork roll egg and cheese sandwich to a young man at my deli, who had never had one before. "What are you doing, Bubbles?" "I am going to bring a sandwich to my dog groomer." It doesn't matter what kind of sandwich it was, we were both making a sandwich delivery at the same time. Everything means something in my world. Sometimes the meaning doesn't become clear until fifty-seven years later, but the meaning eventually makes itself known if you trust the natural order of the universe.

11

JOURNEY TO ME

"When I stand before God at the end of my life, I would hope that I
would not have a single bit of talent left, and could say,
'I used everything you gave me.'"
—Erma Bombeck

Losing yourself to your trauma is like having someone tie you from your feet upside down, hanging from a tree. You spend years wondering if you will ever have that sense of feeling grounded or centered. Disassociation, the feeling of disconnecting from yourself, seems so natural until too many loved ones continue to seek your attention while you are floating somewhere above your body. You go through the motions of working and coming home, making dinner, and floating to the next task in between, wondering if you will ever feel normal again. I didn't know who the hell I was at first. I still don't know how I hid this from my clients, except that listening to others' problems was an escape. Workaholism is a socially acceptable form of addiction, after all.

My originals have been nonexistent and not the least bit supportive or reassuring in all of this, I am told, because they are having their own issues with my discovery. I say, "It is what it is", but that phrase is a cop-out to deny what you are feeling. Sometimes feeling is just too difficult. So, I needed to make it through my brand-new identity crisis, something I thought I was done with back in my early twenties.

For my birthday, I bought myself a dainty necklace in a bright blue color, trimmed in gold. In the center is a cross surrounded by the Star of David. I am Jewish and I am a Christian. I have amped up my Italian cooking, something I was already good at if I say so myself, and I am saying so. I have learned to make polenta, braciola, and long boy stuffed hot peppers. I have made hamantaschen, and we have continued with our bagels and lox for Christmas morning, a tradition I started in the 80s. My maternal side of the family has a connection to pierogies and kielbasa. I have always cooked like that. I used to be one of five children and now I am one of seven. I used to have full siblings and now I have only half siblings.

Twenty years ago, I had a golden retriever mix. Jay and I have always had three rescue dogs and when we lost one this past year, we added a rescue golden retriever to the mix. I could never get another golden retriever until this past year. It was too painful, although I always loved the breed. My original retriever was my soul animal, Kimba. Now we have a new golden; he is blonde, named Simba. Our new pup came with the name, and we did not change it. As a therapist who does sand play therapy, whenever any of the Lion King figures ever showed up in someone's sand tray, especially Simba, it was usually an indicator that someone had father issues. It seemed fitting to our life the day the Mid-Florida Golden Rescue called and told me Simba was available. He seemed a perfect fit for our family. He knows when I am feeling pensive, which is when he jumps up on the couch next to me for a hug and welcomed slobbery kisses.

I made myself vulnerable again, to love. I was fearful of having another golden because of my previous connection to Kimba. Simba is like me. He is an NPE in a family filled with black labs. His blond silky coat stands out and shines. I hope I will someday shine as he does.

Growing up, I played the keyboard and was musically inclined. The DNA test on 23andMe said I most likely did not have an ear for music, which was contrary to how I learned to play the piano by ear. Each time I would sit down to play after that, I made noise, not music. Somewhere in all of that, I told myself that DNA tests are not right about everything. My plan was always to go back to the keyboards when I retired so that I could play piano bar somewhere. Jay bought me a digital piano one Mother's Day, but I had been searching for another one with the plan of getting rid of the dining room table and adding a digital baby grand. After looking for a few years, a thought came to me in the middle of coping with my DNA chaos, that I should go back to my Lowrey organ days. I gave my organ away when we moved to Florida, as it was from the late 70s. I did not think it would make the move. This past year, we purchased a Lowrey Imperial, complete with double keyboard, bass pedals, and a light show that Buzz calls "the spaceship." Jay has been playing too and we now have a combo art room–music room where a formal living and dining room used to be.

My organ was my therapy growing up. I played for hours with the windows open, and regaled the neighbors with Lou Rawls, Billy Joel, Elton John, show tunes and the music from the 40s through 70s. I played the theme from Dr. Zhivago every morning for three months when my maternal grandmother lived with us after my grandfather died. Taking requests was part of my repertoire and my dad would sing with me as his accompanying musician. When we had family gatherings, I did a comedic rendition of "Spanish Eyes" and made my nieces, nephews, friends and family laugh. Somewhere in all of this, I had to find my sense of humor again, too.

Writing was always something that I loved to do. I returned to my writing over the past three years. Historically, I wrote stories in high school and, for most of my life, I kept a journal on and off. Writing has helped me to stay grounded and in touch with my feelings. I blogged about my experiences on www.Ancestry-Discoveries.com which I had hoped would one day be a book. I kept notes in my phone for most of this ride. My cousin, who is also a writer, told me that writing both the blog and this book would uncover a great deal of insight. She was right.

My writing did not stop with journaling. I published an article in the therapy magazine, *In Focus*, which is for mental health therapists in Florida. There is a link in the appendix. This DNA debacle is a recent phenomenon that therapists will have to learn about eventually, as the numbers of us continue to increase. The purpose of the article was to provide education. I also published this past year in a study I spearheaded with two other researchers. The article appeared in the *Journal of Integrative Medicine* on the use of weighted blankets in a mental health hospital to decrease anxiety. The impetus for the study was the high number of autistic people who were admitted and subsequently placed in restraints for meltdowns. The bottom line, if those weighted blankets can help people in the mental health hospital, they could help anyone. I have used my twelve-pound blanket frequently through this DNA discovery.

I also published a chapter in the Social Work Desk Reference this past year called, "Understanding and Treating Autism." That writing came easy to me and it felt like a summary of everything I have learned about autism over the past twenty years. The chapter begins with "The only way to treat autism is with respect." A colleague of mine who was an inspiration to me when I first started out in the autism therapy world, asked me if I would like to co-facilitate workshops. I was beyond honored.

I joined two groups on social media with other NPEs who use the creative arts to express genuine emotions. I have made suncatchers, and I have revisited my love of photography. Jay is an artist. Something that warms my heart is when I take a photograph and Jay likes it and decides he will paint the picture on canvas.

He is a naturally talented artist who never had a lesson in his life. He paints with oils.

I have been collecting funny things about life and have allowed my humor to express itself. For a while, I felt that I had lost it. I found it again. I have a great repertoire for open mic somewhere, sometime soon, and my DNA story has its share of comic twists too. Sometimes I think of life as a series of comic skits that would be perfect for a stand-up show. Larry David could play the wasband, my mother would be played by a Lucille Ball look-alike, Buzz would be played by Rob Reiner, Bob Newhart would play Jay, and for me, I could range in my young to old characters ideally wanting Demi Moore or Debra Winger, but probably ending up with Rosie O'Donnell. My new family would be played by the cast of the Sopranos. We'd have some exceptional skits, and nobody would stop laughing.

I needed desperately to stop hanging on upside down from that tree. I was no longer Swedish and French. I was now Jewish and Italian. I was no longer one of five, I was one of seven. I was a sister and now I am only a half-sister. When Lou Jr. came to visit during one of his reunions with my originals, he called and left a message that it was my "other brother calling." I did not find him funny. I didn't find it kind that he bailed out on seeing me on this trip and was additionally put off when his wife said, "You can come to see us." What I was hearing was in two parts. My half-sisters did a number on his head, and he was not ready or able to enter any realm of conflict, which is standard in my family of origin.

My head still spins when I think about it all, but I can't and won't own any of it. If I have learned one thing from this experience, it was that life is too short. To be less cliché, how I spend my time is how I spend my life. I can't waste another minute when so much of my time and mental energy is taken up by family of origin issues.

I was a big sister now, something I vowed I would do better

than my originals. I would not treat Rebecca like an afterthought or a bother or use her for what I can get like some opportunist. I have enjoyed every second of this part of my experience so far. I took my sister to Radio City Music Hall because that was an event I had shared with my dad every Christmas which brought me great joy. I wanted to share this seasonal delight with my "little sister."

I booked myself tickets to New Jersey and the day of the event arrived. We took a lot of pictures and were both excited to be doing this. Rebecca and I were planning on taking the bus in the morning, seeing the show, going to Rockefeller Center for lunch, and I thought it would be fun to walk through Bryant Park, a place that is lit up, has wonderful shops, and has a magical feel in the air. The first words out of Rebecca's mouth were, "What time are we coming home?" Her husband told her, "Don't piss on Alexandra's parade." Rebecca didn't, but we had not even gotten to New York yet.

Rebecca and I had champagne and walked around the magnificent Radio City Music Hall lobby with its shiny golden banisters, crystal chandeliers and red carpeting. She ran into one of Moshe's friends. Shortly thereafter the texting began, asking her what she was doing in New York. Moshe knew she was not a fan of the city. I also believed he knew who she was with. Now she was clearly out of her comfort zone. Rebecca tensed up a few times, but we did not let that spoil our day. It was, after all, our day. After the show was over, we walked arm-in-arm through crowds of holiday Big Apple dwellers to Rockefeller Center. We were clearly not the only ones with this plan. It was mobbed between the area of Radio City and Rockefeller Center. "I can't believe you talked me into going to New York City, sis." Despite Rebecca's feelings about New York City, she went for me. Trying to sound protective and reassuring, I promised, "Bubbles, I would throw myself in front of a bus for you." I thought that might ease her mind and maybe it did, but I doubt it. We took our obligatory selfie in front of the tree at Rockefeller Center and moved on to find a spot for lunch (on the way to the bus back to New Jersey because I could tell Rebecca was still nervous).

After some hot Irish coffee and lunch, we checked out the time of the next bus. It was later than we thought, so we could walk through Bryant Park. Rebecca is not a traveler or an adventurer. She enjoys the creature comforts and proximity to the area in New Jersey where she is most comfortable. I teased her about taking a trip to Israel, something I have wanted to do my whole life. That will never happen, but it was fun to tease her.

Having been around younger nieces and nephews who were like siblings, it felt natural to have a "little" sister. Perhaps I really didn't change that much. Everything changed around me, but I still feel like me. I am a different me. I feel more free.

12

Connecting to Other NPEs

"Beauty is not who you are on the outside, it is the wisdom and time you gave away to save another struggling soul like you."
—Shannon L. Adler

Moses was the first NPE. There, I said it because it is true. Comically, in the beginning, I sometimes envisioned myself in biblical robes with a beard parting the seas. All that power coming from all that pain, imagine that. But I'm not Moses. My days of rescuing are over. Working through all the conflicting feelings in this process is a work in progress. The only one I can rescue is myself. Some days are better than others. My dad's twenty-year death anniversary approached while I was writing, and I succumbed to the same level of sadness I felt that day when I kissed him goodbye.

I have followed several support groups throughout this journey. When I was in my earlier stages, I was so raw, I made jokes about my experience. I told my story to my first support group and then made jokes to help me navigate the ride. This went over like a fart in church, as Jay would say. I remember one of my first posts said, "I hate my family, maybe I can find another one." One person came to my defense stating that people use humor to cope, but it was rough, as you are standing naked in a room full of people with every raw emotion you have. You function. You inhale and exhale. If you can remember to breathe, that is always a plus. I did not intend to be insensitive. I desired nothing more than a cathartic release of every emotion that was swirling through my being.

I felt so alone all the time, no matter who was in the room with me or who emailed me, called me, or texted to say hello. My originals were never in that picture. I was paranoid to share too much on social media in the various groups because I was fearful that my story would end up on Maury Povich, because some group moderator was being interviewed by some television star. I stuck with the corner market type folks whose jaws dropped but said nothing, as it was safer than being exposed by a group moderator proud to announce they were on a talk show. Participants in some of the groups announced that these folks could be their voice. I fought for my own voice, my whole damn life. I wanted to own my own story and tell it with my own damn voice. There was no way I wanted someone else to tell my story, something that was inevitable with the gossip I heard about after I started to speak my truth. "Nobody puts baby in the corner" (a classic quote from Dirty Dancing).

My trust in humanity waned. I even stopped following some of the support groups out of fear. The numbers of people in my groups kept increasing. As a mental health professional, I was asked to offer help, but I could not do it. I had too much healing to do first. I knew I would know when the time was right for me to help others on this journey. I learned from my caregiver days that the helper puts on the oxygen mask first if the air pressure on the plane drops. At times, I felt like a kamikaze.

I read stories about late discovery adoption, artificial insemination (some call donor conceived), NPEs who had siblings who were ghosting them, original families who were supportive, original families who abandoned their siblings, what not to say, what to say, cries for help, cries on how to forgive. Cries about mothers who were narcissistic which I could not relate to, but I read to educate myself. Joyous reunions of siblings who never met each other, joyous reunions and sometimes films of fathers playing with their adult daughters in childlike settings or sharing meals. There was so much grief and so much glory and so much love.

I learned I wasn't the only person stalking social media for hints, which made me feel less like a voyeuristic threat who would be turned in to the authorities. I learned that one of the most important things I could do was share and then to comment on other posts when people needed comfort and that same sense of normal that I craved, especially in the beginning.

My first presentation on the topic was to a group of clinical social workers in hopes that telling my story would help me to begin healing. Buzz came the day I presented for moral support. It was touching. A colleague who I mentored sat in the front row and cried her eyes out. I thought I needed courage and though I have presented on other topics, this was one of the scariest, intimidating topics I could have possibly talked about. Some found my presentation alarming, intriguing, annoying (clinicians don't self-disclose, which made the whole thing intimidating for me), and one or two felt validated, including me. I was thanked by several participants for sharing. It was truly a vulnerable, unadulterated three hours. I told my story, my truth, to a room full of therapists fearing I would be judged for my disclosure in spite of explaining my reasons. I wanted to help people, but I had to tell my story first.

A woman who resulted from artificial insemination came up to me afterwards and told me she had worked at a hospital with her biological father on the same floor, and that she didn't know he was her father until after he died. Another man turned very pale, quickly, as his grandchild was born because of artificial insemination, and he was fearful that the child would want to find her biological parents someday. This DNA concept is so new that even four years ago, the fear of disclosure was not something people thought about. There can be consent forms signed that provide good faith "no contact" orders, but the fact of the matter is, the child born may feel differently. There are several ethical dilemmas that come out of this situation. I know my parents did not know about DNA and it was probably the farthest thing from anyone's mind. My mother left hints though, such as my biological father's picture cut out of the newspaper. Hints were something she was famous for.

I presented at a retreat for NPEs on healing the inner child and was asked for a repeat performance. My inner child needed healing and reckoning with this situation. I had hoped I could help others with this since, as it was pointed out to me, I came into this DNA surprise after being a part of so much therapy, along with having developed years of coping through my other life scenarios.

I have uncovered so many other NPEs along the way. One of the first I can recall in this present day was my hairdresser. I had just come back from Hawaii, and I shared with her during my first haircut back that I have gorgeous cousins, some of whom I met for the first time. I break out my Ancestry app and make my announcement on a subsequent trip. Frankie, my hairdresser, asks how my gorgeous cousins are and I tell her one of the first things Jay said to me after this discovery was, "We are never going to Hawaii again." It was fun to see him be a little jealous, and it was probably his way of making jokes. Frankie still makes jokes about my gorgeous cousins and Jay's response to "never" going back to Hawaii. Fast forward another six months and I find myself in the shop again to hear the story that Frankie had a new sister, compliments of her DNA "just for fun" exploration.

I recalled two people from my past who found out their dads were not their biological fathers, either. One was a friend I met on vacation every year who was my pen pal in-between trips to Maine each summer. Lani and I spent two days together here in Florida and she shared her news. She had figured out why her dad stopped talking with her after her parents divorced. Then there was my son Buzz's godmother who, as an adult, also found out that her dad was not her biological father over thirty years ago, someone she called uncle was.

I was volunteering at a golf outing in Lecanto, Florida, about a month into my discovery. With raw, but masked emotion, I worked all day setting up, delivering water to the golfers, and kibitzing with the other volunteers. It was fun, and I loved driving the golf cart since I have never golfed in my entire life except for miniature golf. My friend Rene and her husband Jimmy were both present. Jimmy is about twenty years Rene's senior. They both have Boston accents but have lived in Florida for over twenty years. Jimmy makes the greatest pizza and credits his dad, the Boston pizza man, with his innate skills.

About a year later, Rene called and asked me to meet her for lunch. With the app open to Ancestry, she told me that Jimmy was devastated. You guessed it, he found out at eighty-two that his dad was not his biological father. Like me, Jimmy had an idyllic perception of his dad. I can tell you the transformative effects it had on Jimmy were not positive. It is not information he was ready to share with anyone and it was clear for several years after that Jimmy continues to feel devastated, barely able to discuss the matter. Jimmy will talk with me about it, but only after a great deal of probing. I believe he continues to struggle, living in shock.

Rene recently called me with wonderful news. Jimmy had a reprieve from his sadness recently when his "new nieces and nephews" wanted to connect with him. They were meeting on Zoom that afternoon. Jimmy knew their father. He shared old neighborhood stories with his new half-brother's family. The connection lifted his spirits and Rene agreed that the call helped Jimmy along on his healing journey.

Jay, Buzz and I recently returned from a two-week vacation in the Keys. While we were there and waiting for dinner one night,

I struck up a conversation with a woman who was also waiting. Vacation and a glass of wine loosened my lips, and I told her my story. Her eyes widened and she gave me a hug. This young lady told me her story about being artificially inseminated, finding out through Ancestry that she had Jewish DNA. Her mother will not speak to her about it. Her husband thanked me for sharing and said he felt like we were meant to meet since his wife was carrying a great deal of pain and was forced to suffer in silence. We are still in touch. I have also vowed to keep sharing my story in hopes that not only will it help me to continue to heal but also to help others to share their stories. And share, they did.

Pastor Joe told me a story a long time ago about a man at the Jersey Shore who resulted from a baby selling situation back in the late 50s. He was told he was adopted at his father's funeral and later wrote a book about it. I read the book in a day and connected on so many levels since he fell under the category of late discovery adoption in spite of the fact that his adoption was not legal. The author and I have been in touch. He works in the town that I lived in prior to our move to Florida.

Recently, I had lunch with an NPE who lives nearby. She shared her story of searching for her biological father in Europe. Her mom is still alive and told her who her father was. She was named after him! This same friend connected marvelously with siblings across several continents. Then, she took a DNA test only to have her world shattered when she found out her new family was not biologically connected. Her mom was wrong about who her father was. The plot thickens yet again. She is meeting her new sister in Europe soon and has already met her brother. It was even more surprising to hear that her husband is an NPE too, and he was on pins and needles waiting for responses from messages and emails to his biological family while I was writing this book.

Jay and I had contractors in our home recently for a project we are working on. I shared my story with two of the three contractors. I looked up one of the contractor's names on Ancestry and he had family in the same province in Sicily where my family comes from. The final visit from that contractor yielded even more surprising results. I shared my story and the fact that my book was almost finished. Jay and I heard within two hours and a much-extended visit, that he discovered he had a daughter eight years ago. He was shocked.

It took him six months to spring the news on his wife. She knew anyway since there were pictures sent by the child's mother. There was no denying the dad and child were related, she looked just like him. You can only imagine how floored this contractor was when he finally told his wife and she admitted that she was waiting for him to confide in her. He did not know what to do about it. His wife replied, "If you wait any more to do something about it, we are going to have a problem."

Apparently, his daughter was conceived while he and his wife split up and he moved out-of-state. His daughter carried a different man's name on her birth certificate. This birth certificate father was considered her legal father and there were no DNA rights to this child. The child's biological dad desired to be part of his daughter's life. He pursued this in court and was turned down because legally, DNA did not matter. The child's birth certificate father died. The child's mom kept her and her biological father apart and told the eight-year-old that he was her stepfather when a court finally granted visitation rights. This is parental alienation at its finest and yes, the topic of another book. His daughter is now living with him, his wife, and her new sisters.

During my writing, I received a phone call from an older loved one who wanted to share that she had "skeletons in her closet, too." Seventy years ago, she gave a baby up for adoption. She never told a soul except for her husband. She described sleepless nights and worry and did not pursue her child because she was afraid he might not have made it (he was very jaundiced at birth). They have since connected. Her heart is open, and her adult children were welcoming and excited that they have a brother. My loved one went on to tell me that her daughter's friend found out that her biological father was the man next door.

Jay and I sat at the bar having dinner and ESPN was on telling the story about Barry Breman. Barry Breman was a salesman from Michigan and was known as "The Great Imposter." He posed as a Major League Baseball umpire in the World Series, and a referee in the National Football League. He practiced in uniform with the NBA, posed as a Dallas Cowboys Cheerleader, and the list goes on. Well, Barry was a busy boy and evidently frequented sperm banks. So far, according to Wikipedia, he has at least forty children.

The list goes on. My head spins when I stop to think about it. Reading or hearing so many stories, in the various family secrets capacity, finds me feeling overwhelmed at times. Other times, it is extremely validating. Whether people are longing to connect with newly discovered fathers who are married to jealous wives, or wives who were betrayed, or wives who are compliant with status quo, NPEs who are longing to connect with new siblings who refuse to acknowledge their existence, or original siblings who lack compassion, to donor conceived individuals who long to connect with families they already know on a cellular level, there are many scenarios. The characteristic which causes us all to bond is hiraeth, or simplistically, connection.

My journey and my struggles continue. There are weeks when I am fine (Fine is an acronym for fucked up, insecure, neurotic, and emotional). There are other weeks when I am excited and happy and feel beyond blessed. Sometimes I feel guilty for feeling excited and happy and beyond blessed. The healing has been progressing. My situation is something I will never get over, but thanks to the love and support of Jay, Rebecca, and my family, I am getting through. I don't want to forget my dad and our connection, and I don't want to miss anything in the time I have left in my life.

I have reconciled myself to forgoing the trip to Sweden and

Montreal. I loved Italy when I toured back in the 80s and have always wanted to go back. Now I would add a trip to Sicily. Perhaps that voyage to Israel is still in the cards, though this time, it would be with a purpose. My paternal grandmother came from Balkan Jewish roots, so that would take care of the sojourn to Poland, taking care of Lithuania and Latvia in the process, which connects to my mother's family of origin. Of course, Aunt Rosie's birthday is coming up, and perhaps a hug from an elderly aunt in New Jersey would do the trick. Connection, it's all about connection, connecting to others, and connecting to myself.

13
—

BE WHO YOU ARE

"Perhaps this is the moment for which you were created."
—Esther 4:14

I was working on this book on a bright and crisp spring morning in Florida. It was unseasonably cool for this time of year. There is still something missing that needs to be said that will help others, indicated by the nagging feeling I had with me for the past several weeks. Jay and I were dealing with a very ill golden retriever with IMHA, a life-threatening anemia. For the past month, we were on the proverbial roller coaster ride, teetering between life and death. Believe it or not, despite the two of us taking turns watching his chest move gently up and down and more labored than I would like, I have learned the art of riding over one roller coaster at a time. Simba is the blessing who we rescued last year, the one who was to help bring me back to who I was. This was the "person" I have searched for over the past four years. Who am I now, was a constant perseveration which invaded my dreams and haunted daytime fleeting moments when I should have been attending to something else. I was driven and on a mission to take this external discovery of mine and see what it meant to me internally, on a much deeper level. Everything I saw or did has taken on existential significance in the world of my crisis.

The pandemic was a mixed blessing. As much as I hated being forced to stay home with limited contact to the outside world, it forced me to take the occasion to explore myself and the people around me. I had to be coming out of this DNA haze four years later because I was caring how my new existence in the lives of my new family affected them. Sometimes worry would creep in on how this DNA discovery has affected my relationship with my husband. I always hated the question in its repetition, "who are you?" I thought I always knew. I often thought the same thoughts anyone who endures a trauma has. Why me and why now?

I am flooded with responses during my prayer and meditation time. Why not you? Why not now? Everything that has happened to me in my life has not been about me, although I sometimes tell Jay, "But I am the center of the universe." I had several conversations with my ninety-two-year-old aunt. We have become the greatest of friends through all of this. Somehow my intuition, when it wasn't clouded with tears and grief, always knew this might happen. Aunt Rosie told me more than once that my existence has brought an additional dimension to her life. I am honored. Hearing this from a congressional candidate and political advocate who stood on the court steps in Trenton, NJ with her fist in the air organizing on behalf of the Equal Rights Amendment was profound.

Perhaps in summing up this experience, *profound* is the perfect word. Throughout most of my adult life, I have asked in prayer for direction and guidance no matter what my undertaking was. Whether it was suffering through a statistics class as a prerequisite for graduate school, or deciding to specialize in autism in my practice, I have always "been led". I usually have listened. Like anyone, anywhere, at any time, my path leads me into a clearing in the woods to stop and look and sometimes breathe, at something else. Am I being tested? Was there cause to question that I have done this for twenty years and now something else is in the cards?

After sending a picture of my orchids to Aunt Lori, I received a response telling me she had plans to grow orchids when she retired. Aunt Lori is thirteen years older than I am. She is the social worker who lived in the next town who several people told me about, who looked like me. Aunt Lori went further to tell me she always wanted to write a book, which I am, and grow orchids, which I did. Aunt Lori said, "you are like my actualization." As the words were appearing on my cell phone, I was seeing the quote from the book of Esther, "Perhaps this was the moment for which you were created." This felt like radical acceptance, unconditional love, an answer to my feelings of hiraeth.

Rebecca and I speak by phone or text message daily, even if it is just to say hello. We both lead busy lives but are never too busy to answer a call or send a text message back. Sometimes I felt like I didn't matter in the world of my originals as text messages went unanswered or gatherings went on without me. It feels good to matter to someone who proudly calls me her "sis." Sometimes I think Rebecca doesn't believe this whole discovery happened either. Sometimes I feel we are in a continuous process of navigating our relationship. We were not in each other's lives while growing up. Rebecca has welcomed me with open arms and an open heart and for that warm embrace, I am particularly comforted when my grief comes to call.

I found out through asking questions and listening to contexts of conversation that my biological father had traveled the road to a mental health facility for detoxification and alcoholism. Since addiction is born in traumatic experiences, I would bet that my coming into this world may have contributed to his suffering. That is not my fault. The wondering began if Frank knew about me. Rebecca supplied me with the name of three of his girlfriends prior to his death. As I mentioned, one of the three spoke with me. Ruth was so concerned about my perceptions of Frank. I immediately admitted my own knowledge of his alcoholism. Ruth said that he was a "functioning alcoholic." Ruth told me that he called her husband to let him know what was going on. Frank did not want to be alone. Frank battled cancer, Frank battled alcoholism, and Frank battled bipolar disorder. She told me that most people did not know he was drinking early in the morning and that she would scold him for drinking because of his cancer. I am still learning and putting pieces of my life's puzzle together. The story Ruth shared was that Frank was leaving for somewhere, sometime, between Thanksgiving and Christmas. When asked where he was going, Frank replied, "I am going to see my daughter. I have not seen her since she was a baby. I hope she will talk to me." That fits my man in the mall timeline. Ruth shared that Frank told her I wanted nothing to do with him. Now was he speaking about me, or is there another Barrie baby around? Sometimes I feel like there may be another sister out there. I promised Rebecca I would help her through it if that were the truth. If Frank was talking about me, it just wasn't true. Sometimes we tell ourselves lies to cope with the pain of our reality. It would be ideal to have had this conversation with Frank myself. The rescuer in me believes he might still be here. It had to have had a direct effect on his relationship with my sister and brother.

This DNA discovery experience is likened to the puzzle being completed and almost ready for decoupage. Suddenly you realize there is a piece missing or the piece you thought went in one spot did not quite fit. But the earthquake hits and the puzzle falls off the table and becomes unglued, scattering puzzle pieces all over the rug while some fly under the sofa with the dust bunnies in the corner. The puzzle needs to be put back together again, hopefully with the pieces not too bent or soiled and easily reconnected. This is not a process that happens overnight. Carefully figuring out where each piece of the puzzle fits will take time and patience to enjoy the beauty and perhaps the new artistic creation. Suddenly, it wasn't a picture of that covered bridge in Pennsylvania down the road from grandma's house anymore. But perhaps this turns out to be Michelangelo's Sistine Chapel.

This is the true nature of trauma, reinvention, redefining, rediscovery. The puzzle makes sense. While putting all those colorful pieces together, sometimes another bombshell is dropped that has nothing to do with your DNA and everything to do with life just happening around you. When our golden retriever got sick less than a year after he rescued me, an immediate reaction was to connect him to my past, my search for myself. As we are hoping, praying, giving him the dreaded prednisone with blood transfusions, etc., I realized that the part of me that joined with Jay to be his loving caregivers was always a part of who I am. I'm still me. Here is hoping I got the message, and the illness our Simba endures will go away.

As a therapist, when working with trauma clients, sometimes I use sand play. Sand play is based in Jungian psychology. The figures used for expression are called "archetypes." An archetype is a universally understood symbol. It is up to each individual to build a world in the sand. Disney is filled with archetypes. I have many Disney characters that people have used through the years in their projective sand play. I always felt bad for the clients when Simba showed up in their tray. Perhaps my subconscious was connecting to my own father issues that were not part of my awareness yet.

My first golden retriever was named Kimba (named after the white lion on a cartoon I watched after school). Our recent addition is named Simba, after the main character of The Lion King. He came with that name. Our first golden retriever was red. Simba is white. It took two weeks for me to stop calling him Kimba. The original owners had a child with autism. Simba was purchased to be a service animal providing therapeutic support. Apparently, I was told, Simba did not bond with the child. But he bonded with me, and I work with individuals with autism. It most likely would have caused a financial hardship for a young family going back and forth to therapy, as IMHA is expensive to treat. I could not even imagine what it would have been like for the child and his family to endure the difficulties of life and death of a loved pooch who is part of the family. I was glad it happened to us and not to Simba's original family. Jay is sometimes involved with my work as he teaches art, and he helps with some of my office events. This time, Jay and I were still indirectly taking care of a family, most likely akin to the families I deal with every day.

Grief and trauma were not foreign to me. Organizing and moving the energy was something I was used to. Yet, there have been more moments than not that I have completely denied I was traumatized. I heard the many platitudes, "Your dad is still your dad," "He's still your father," and any sentence that started with, "It doesn't matter…" caused me to completely disassociate from the conversation. Trauma will do that to you. Disassociation is part of the trauma journey. I probably drank too much wine at the beginning of this journey. That fosters disassociation and impedes healing. I worked extra hours, and I ate too much. You don't have to feel if you are working and listening to everyone else's challenges. Your own feelings are numbed to reality. Wine does that too. Emotional eating is second nature to me, and I have told myself it is a lot healthier than wine. As for the workaholism, a trait I inherited from my mother, society rewards this type of behavior.

Having a short temper, road rage, defensive behavior, caregiving too much, checking out, disorganization, fuzzy thinking, rage without cause, hypervigilance, shame, depression, anger, flashbacks, overthinking, over feeling, not feeling (numbing), guilt, anxiety, sleeplessness, sleeping too much, body aches, muscle aches, tachycardia, crying, headaches, are only a few of the lovely signs of trauma. I admit, some of these beauties were part of my experience. Perhaps all of them. As we go through this discovery, we are carrying a lifelong list of traumatic events.

I immersed myself in reading the stories of others, especially once the numbness subsided and I ate healthier. Telling my story to others has helped and the writing, including my blog, has been a creative outlet and a godsend. The creative arts are a constructive way to cope through this struggle. I have made Christmas ornaments, redecorated our home, turned to music, baked beads to make sun catchers, planted flowers, and have cooked creative recipes that I had never made in my life.

I have used my weighted blanket on the days when I am out of sorts, made time to get into nature, enjoyed the wind chimes on my back patio along with the pond with its waterfall. We had fairies in our yard, I always said. This was something that made me fall in love with our home. I felt like the fairies had left the building, so to speak. But little by little, I can sense those beacons of light around our gardens again. So, those feelings of well-being do come back. It just takes time and it can be inconsistent. Such is the course of trauma. There are good days, great days. Then the lights dim, and you are back in the abyss again. But then the next day arrives, and the cycle continues. If you are like me, the bad days are fewer and far between. The days when I am in that rut, that abyss, I let it be. Jay leaves me alone and I promise him that if I am chewing glass, it is not about him. He is too patient with me.

While writing this memoir, there have been some minor miracles. Jay and I are on full time cycles of care for our Simba. As I write, at first I am frustrated because our perfectly coiffed lawn, thanks to Jay, has not been kept up. But when I stop and look closer, the weeds look like daisies. Daisies were my mom's favorite flower, Aunt Charlene's too. I feel like every day I see those daisy weeds that are growing wild, I receive a warm and gracious hello from heaven.

Taking the time to relax after a long day, I sit on the couch with the doors wide open, bringing in the fresh, cool air from the backyard. I spot a cardinal in the tree. Another hello, this time, from my dad. I am not alone. You are not alone. The best way to get through this DNA Discovery is to go through it. Go through it while being kind to yourself. On the other side of this, you will be waiting. You are still you. You will not feel that way at the outset. Eventually, with time and patience, you will be whole again, but your complete self will be different, renewed, unique.

People ask me if I had to do it over again, would I have taken that DNA test for fun? The answer is simple. The answer is yes. Why, you ask? Because I would not have met my sister and my new family. I would not have felt this new love and connection I have in my life. I would not have connected to who I really am. It takes work, patience, trust, faith, hope, and love. As the good book says, the greatest of these is love.

EPILOGUE: FOR NPES – A WORD ON REJECTION

REJECTION: IT'S NOT ABOUT YOU

*"You are a child of the universe, no less than the trees
and the stars, you have a right to be here."*
—Max Ehrmann

A year into my discovery, I blogged about my brother, Moshe. I made light of his rejection towards me. I posted a picture of my favorite Halloween skeleton wearing an Uncle Sam hat sipping out of a yard of margarita glass with the words, "This is me waiting for my brother to call." My sense of humor was always one of my favorite defense mechanisms. The fact is this rejection seems to be common with NPEs in one form or another. Knowing you are not alone helps, but it does not take away the painful sadness of the, albeit irrational, "You don't even know me, why don't you like me?" feelings.

I received emails to my blog asking me why siblings reject newly found brothers and sisters without even knowing them. It feels like someone is assigning fault to innocent parties. Sometimes people will ask me why Moshe won't talk to me, as if I have the answers. One of my cousins shared Moshe thought I wanted money. Now anyone who knows me knows I have never been about the money and to even suggest such a thing is offensive.

Initially, I could understand that rationale, but after several years of not asking anyone for anything, other than the time of day, the money question should have been answered by now.

To be totally transparent, I tell myself the lie that it doesn't bother me, but it does. We were at dinner one night and my sister's friend was probing about what she called our "Maury Povich" situation. Somehow it felt as though someone was gaslighting me, when she looked at me and bluntly announced that I was bitter. I was speechless and didn't answer her. I felt judged, and I vowed I would never be in her company again. Frankly, if I need to be bitter to get through it, then that is what I need to do. But bitter was enormously larger than life at one time and I promised myself not to stay there too long. It is part of the healing process to wallow in whatever it is we feel rather than stuffing it down and denying the feelings that we possess.

Throughout this process, it is not unusual to feel judged or have people make what they perceive to be helpful observations. These people are not you and they don't know your experience, and they cannot expect you to just "get over it." You will never get over it. You will hopefully, with the right support system, get through it. Connection with those supports is your path to healing.

Rejection takes many forms in this journey of ours. There are some NPEs who were rejected by biological fathers, birth certificate fathers, siblings from their original families, and their new siblings and, sadly, their own mothers. A bright idea came to me that perhaps I should research and publish the answer to the question, why do people reject their new relatives? But I realized that none of the people who are doing the ghosting would agree to such an interview. What's wrong with people?

It sucks that first you are traumatized by this DNA news, as I was, and you would hope for some kindness and compassion from individuals who are related to you. Whether it is a father, mother, birth certificate father, or siblings (originals and new ones), it hurts. Sadly, there are other members of the new branches of our family tree who we might never connect to, in my case, nephews, who are minors.

It feels like you are being shunned. It feels like you are alienated. It hurts.

The lack of response and callousness of other people is not about you. Of course, we all take it personally and if you need to do that to work through it that is why God made journals, support groups, and therapists, not in order of importance, of course. We have no control over other people's crappy behavior or thought process. This goes for our families, friends, and anyone else we encounter in our lives. When it comes right down to it, we have very little control at all. You may have no power over others' reactions or responses, but you have the power to control your own reactions and responses. To heal, we need both. Personally, when I can control my own reactions, I am usually pretty satisfied and proud of myself. Jay and I have a saying that we adopted over the years: "Why not sleep on it?" That puts distance between you and your reactions to whatever the problem is at hand, not to mention the much-needed sleep you have been lacking because of all you carry on your shoulders.

There will always be well-meaning people around you who try to make you feel better. Don't get me wrong, they are your people. To get through this, you need to honor your own feelings first. Jay is usually forewarned when this occurs. "Jay, I am so angry I need to chew glass and it's not about you." Jay, the some-times-sainted husband of mine, usually clears the area and leaves me alone. Sometimes he will ask me if I need a hug, and other times, he leaves me on my own to be in the emotions that seem to intrude out of nowhere. Anger, in and of itself, is complicated and never alone. Usually, if you check in with yourself about your anger and feel around inside your psyche, you will discover anger is holding hands with another feeling like sadness, guilt, shame, or a host of others. Sometimes sad looks mad. I find that is true for me at least.

It is okay to feel what you feel. It is not okay to react by taking it out on others and misdirect the confusion towards people who care about you. My go to medium is writing. Throughout this or any other traumatic journey, keep a journal. There are millions of journal prompts on social media and through search engines. My Pinterest box is filled with prompts. When all else fails, write letters to the creeps who are injuring your soul in your journal, but never mail the letters. Those are your gut level reactions. Letter writing in a journal is an effective way to maintain focus. It addresses the excuse we all use from time to time, "I don't know what to write about." Writing a letter of encouragement to your-self helps too. Start the letter with, "Dear (self-name), I love you and I want you to know…" My cousin, a prolific writer, assured me at the beginning of my book authorship that I would uncover a great deal of wisdom if I would take the pen to the paper. Writing forced me to face things I really avoided, and it brought me revelations and insight. Sometimes, I would laugh at my own jokes because I believe I am funny, but I would also force myself to look at the humor and ask, what pain am I trying to avoid?

Sometimes, I would stop writing (or keep going depending on how my intuition guided me) as I faced my sad demons, some-times with tears, a lot of tears. I drew strength from every musical note I played when I pounded away at the keyboards. Art, as crafts or painting garden gnomes, cooking, or planting flowers, were wonderful diversions and emotional outlets. There is some-thing to be said about spending time out in nature, digging in the dirt. Find your creative mode of expression and you will be helped. Hope for slow and steady progress. Saying you are okay after a few weeks is not being true to yourself. You deserve the truth after you have been lied to your whole life, don't you? You can start by being honest with yourself first. Make some quiet time to listen to your heart. Your heart knows what is true.

I mentioned already the exclusion from my original siblings. While going through this trauma of my own, memories seep into my awareness from time to time and more pieces to my puzzle are put together. Years ago, for example, I recalled family vacations that my father's siblings had every year in Palm Springs. My dad's siblings and their spouses would gather, and all go to a condo there. I said nothing to my parents, but I thought it was hurtful that my mom and dad were not included. I wonder now if it is because there was "adult talk" while I was growing up that I was not my dad's biological daughter. It felt like my dad's family did not like my mother, which somehow translated to rejection of the child that I was. Rejection directly triggers the inner child who lives within us. That child within all of us carries a lifetime of childhood memories, both positive and negative, that were observed and felt but never expressed.

Lack of inclusion has been a major trigger for me my whole life. Perhaps that is why I easily advocate for those who are excluded. I over-invite to parties. At my first wedding, the music played, "I Love a Parade" instead of "Here Comes the Bride" because I had twenty people in my wedding party. I didn't want anyone to feel left out.

It is a wise idea to examine triggers so that you learn, when they come out of left field, you can talk yourself through them. If someone tells me I trigger them, they hate my response, "Nobody is responsible for your triggers, but you." When a strong feeling emerges for you in these familial situations, connect to the feeling. Name what those feelings are that you are experiencing. Are you feeling angry, scared, lonely, sad, guilty, shame, or more than one? Close your eyes. Where do you feel those experiences in your body? When was another time in your life when you felt exactly the same way? Now journal about it. Close your eyes again and allow yourself to relax and take time for deep breaths, followed by gentle breathing.

After a few minutes, you will hopefully feel more connected to yourself. I like to get under my weighted blanket for twenty minutes. The research shows that twenty minutes under a weighted blanket that weighs ten percent of your body weight decreases anxiety. You can also take warm baths in lavender, baking soda, and Epsom salt. If you believe, you can also pray. Prayer works. Find what works for you. Make a toolbox of survival tips on your phone that you can draw from anytime you need to. I believe in you. You've got this.

Self-awareness of triggers can make a difference between reacting and responding. Reacting comes from gut level emotion, usually brought on by triggers. Responding is connecting to those triggers, understanding where they are coming from, making yourself stop, breathe, and think before you act. It will make a difference. Hopefully, it will be that your outcomes are more positive for you. If you have a trusted friend or loved one you can vent to, that helps in the responding process. Speak your reactions to your trusted friend or support group and then give yourself time before you respond. Triggering events have the unquestionable potential to re-traumatize your already wounded soul. Your feelings are valid. When your experiences offer you powerful emotions in waves, wax down your surfboard and ride the wave. You may end up on the shore after swallowing what feels like the entire ocean, or maybe the board will hit you on the head. The journey from wave to shore is temporary. But you will eventually get to shore. This is your narrative. Write it your way.

One parting thought. Keep your eyes on what is positive. In my case, I have an ending that is positive. I fell in love with several people in my new family and we have established relationships that differ from my life prior to my discovery. Aunt Rosie would say, "There is an additional dimension to life now." As adults, we come into this experience with our own hopeful expectations, whether it is to get a health history, or form new connections to help us heal. We are not new to family relationships and their potential benefits and drawbacks. We are seasoned and experienced already. Focus on what is working. Perhaps it may not be your familial connections if that did not happen, but maybe you have forged friendships and camaraderie with people you never would have met if this experience did not happen. What you focus on grows. The choice is up to you.

PHOTO ALBUM

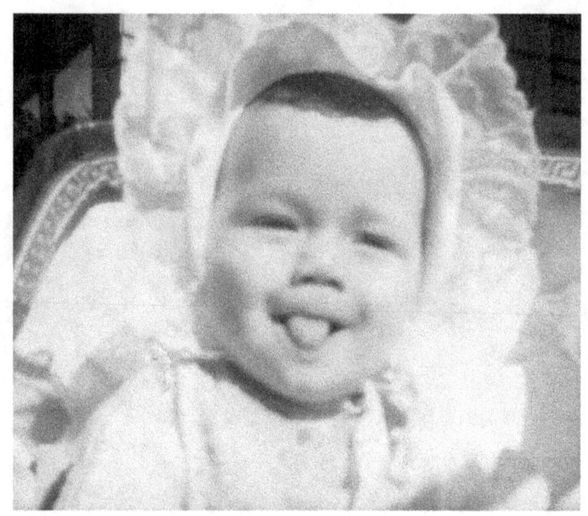

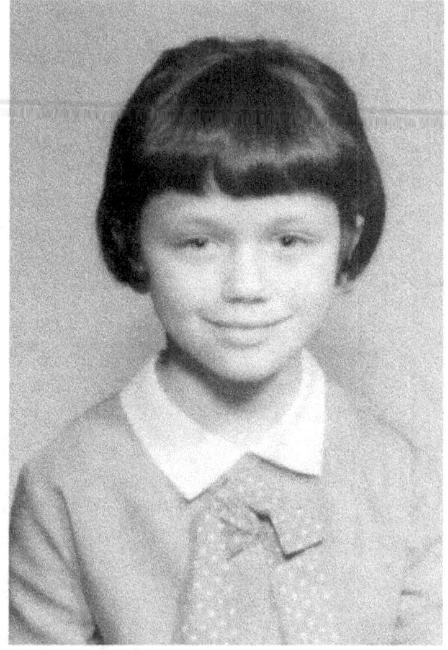

Am I cute or what?

Me and Mom Irene

Me and Dad Lou Sr.

Lou Sr. and Irene

*Me and Dad on my
Wedding Day Dancing to
"Daddy's Little Girl"*

*First Picture I saw of my
Biological Father*

Frank Barrie

*Father Frank with
My Grandfather*

*Aunt Charlene, My Grandmother,
Bio Father Frank*

*Hamantaschen Party: Vic,
Lyndsey, Anna, Me, Rebecca,
Aunt Charlene, Aunt Rosie*

My First Hanukkah

*Cousin Lyndsey, Aunt Charlene
and Me*

*Me and Rebecca at Radio City
Music Hall*

First Time I Met my Sister Rebecca, May 17, 2018

Aunt Samantha, Aunt Lori and Me
Meeting for the First Time

Jay, Me and Buzz

Me and Buzz

Me and Jay

Appendix — Resources

Author, Annette Becklund's information:
www.AncestryDiscoveries.com – Follow the blog
www.AnnetteLBecklund.com – Professional web page
Spotify playlist: Ancestry Discoveries NPE MPEs [Lyrics are not in the book due to copywrite laws but the story in music can be found on Spotify.]

Article: "DNA Discoveries: What Happens Under the Sheets Doesn't Stay There Forever"
https://issuu.com/fmhca/docs/aug_2020

Community Organizations
Coalition for Genetic Truth
Facebook: https://www.facebook.com/genetictruth
Twitter: @GeneticTruth
Instagram: @genetic_truth

Right to Know Organization – https://righttoknow.us/
Right to Know is a non-profit that advocates for people impacted by DNA surprises and misattributed parentage which can occur due to an adoption, assisted conception, or those conceived from a non-paternal event (NPE) through education, mental health initiatives, and advocacy to ensure our fundamental human right to know our genetic identity. Each month we hold an on-line group discussion with a licensed therapist and an educational webinar, check out our events page. We maintain a hotline, 323-TALK-MPE, so no one ever feels alone with their discovery (or reach out online). Give us a call, we're here to listen, pair you with a mentor, help you find a therapist, and answer any questions.

Social Media
- Twitter: @RighttoKnowUs
  (https://mobile.twitter.com/righttoknowus/)
- Instagram: @RighttoKnowUs
  (https://www.instagram.com/righttoknowus)
- TikTok: @RighttoKnowUs
  (https://www.tiktok.com/@righttoknowus)
- Facebook: RightToKnowUs
  (https://www.facebook.com/RighttoKnowUS)
- LinkedIn:
  (https://www.linkedin.com/company/right-to-know/)

MPE Counseling Directory
(www.MPECounseling.org)
A list of licensed therapists by state with experience working with people with misattributed parentage. If you do not see a therapist in your state, call 323-TALK-MPE and we'll help you find one.

MPE Education Classes and Informational Videos
(www.MPE-Education.org)
We offer classes and informational videos on topics related to misattributed parentage and DNA surprises. There are also classes available with continuing education credits for licensed therapists.

RTK Peer-Led Facebook Support Groups
DNA Identity Surprise & This MPE Life
(https://www.facebook.com/groups/thismpelife)
This MPE Life is an inclusive support group for individuals with a DNA surprise and those impacted by a Mis-attributed Parental Experience (MPE), geared towards building friendships and encouraging lighthearted banter around our new Life with an MPE.

MPE Cross Cultural Connections from a DNA Surprise (https://www.facebook.com/groups/mpeccc)
MPE CCC is an inclusive, intersectional support group for people with a DNA surprise and those impacted by a Mis-attributed Parentage Experience (MPE) that offers a safe space to share, process, give and receive feedback, pool resources, and have discussions about the experiences, challenges, emotions, and highlighting changes in ethnicity surrounding MPEs.

MPE Jewish Identity & DNA Surprise (https://www.facebook.com/groups/mpejewishidentitysurprise)
MPE Jewish Surprise is an inclusive support group for individuals who through DNA testing have discovered Jewish heritage and in some cases lost it due to a DNA test and is a safe space to share, process, give and receive feedback, pool resources, and have discussions about the full range of experiences, challenges, and emotions of the MPE Jewish journey.

DNA Surprise Support for MPE Family and Friends (https://www.facebook.com/groups/dnasurprisesupport-mpefamilyfriends)
The ripple effects of a DNA surprise can affect so many individuals. This is an inclusive support group for family and friends of individuals impacted by a DNA surprise or a Mis-attributed Parental Experience (MPE).

Facebook Private Groups

Adoptees Only: Found/Reunion The Next Chapter
https://www.facebook.com/groups/1567902216819000

Coalition for Genetic Truth
https://www.facebook.com/genetictruth
Twitter: @GeneticTruth
Instagram: @genetic_truth

DNAngels NPE Support Group
https://www.facebook.com/groups/dnangelssupportgroup
Twitter: @DNAngels4
Instagram: @dnangelsorg

DNA Surprises Support Group
https://www.facebook.com/groups/1798909400175879/

Donor Conceived People, Siblings, Parents, and Donors (Sperm, Egg, Embryo)
https://www.facebook.com/groups/DonorConceived

MPE Cross Cultural Connections
https://www.facebook.com/groups/463672101233690

NPE Only: Togetherness Heals
https://www.facebook.com/groups/npeonly/
Twitter: @NPEsOnly1
Instagram: @npesonly

Severance
(Adoptees, NPEs, Donor-Conceived & Other Identity Seekers)
https://www.facebook.com/groups/402792990448461

Togetherness Heals Peer to Peer Facebook Support Groups
Togetherness Heals—NPE Only
(https://www.facebook.com/groups/npeonly)
Togetherness Heals—NPE Only is a safe haven solely for NPEs, LDAs and Donor Conceived Persons (no family or friends), because "Togetherness Heals." Our peer to peer support groups offer twice weekly Zooms in addition to Facebook support.

Togetherness Heals—Book Club

(https://www.facebook.com/groups/togethernesshealsnpe-bookclub)

Togetherness Heals—Book Club is a safe haven solely for NPEs, Donor Conceived Adults and Adoptees (no family or friends), because Togetherness Heals" The group was formed with NPEs, Donor Conceived Adults, and Adoptees in mind. In this safe container we read, digest, dissect and share books written by and/or for NPEs, Donor Conceived Adults, and Adoptees in various stages of their journeys.

Togetherness Heals—Adoptees Only

(https://www.facebook.com/groups/togethernesshealsadopteesonly)

Togetherness Heals—Adoptees Only is a safe haven solely for Adoptees and LDAs (no family or friends), because "Togetherness Heals." Our peer-to-peer support groups offer twice weekly Zooms in addition to Facebook support.

This MPE Life

https://www.facebook.com/groups/thismpelife

Additional Facebook Support Groups: Adopted Adults Support Group, DNA NPE Friends (with multiple specialty and spin off groups, i.e. Jewish, Over Fifty, Creativity, Photography, Regional); Adoptees, NPEs DC & Other Genetic Identity Seekers; Adult Adoptees Support Adopted People; DNA Surprise Support Group for MPE Family & Friends; Donor Conceived Community Support Group; Donor Conceived People, Siblings, Parents, and Donors; Donor Deceived; Forum for Late Discovery Adoptees; Late Discovery Adoptees & Family; NPE Only: After the Discovery; Unknown Fathers DNA; We are Donor Conceived.

MEDIA
(podcasts and magazines specifically for NPEs/MPEs)

Everything's Relative podcast
Websites:
www.evesturges.la
www.everythingsrelativepodcast.com
https://podcasts.apple.com/us/podcast/everythings-rela-tive-with-eve-sturges/id1459167540
https://podcasts.apple.com/us/podcast/everythings-rela-tive-with-eve-sturges/id1459167540
Facebook: https://www.facebook.com/everythingsrelativepodcast
Instagram: @everythingsrelativepodcast

NPE Guide
https://www.npeguide.com/ Dr. Gina Daniel

NPE Stories podcast
https://podcasts.apple.com/us/podcast/npe-stories/id1464478802
https://open.spotify.com/show/0llQ713NQl025zujkmvD-5V?si=Q29JO5PGSKGnOvJCg61r4w
Instagram: @lilymwood

Severance Magazine
Website: https://www.severancemag.com
Facebook: https://www.facebook.com/severancemag
Twitter: @Severancemag
Instagram: @severancemag

Sex, Lies & The Truth podcast
https://sexliesandthetruth.com
Twitter: @JodiRabb
Instagram: @sexliestruth

SEARCH ANGELS

DNAngels
Website: https://www.dnangels.org
Facebook: https://www.facebook.com/dnangels.org
Twitter: @DNAngels4
Instagram: @dnangelsorg

RETREATS

Hiraeth Hope & Healing (https://www.facebook.com/groups/hiraethhopeandhealing) (www.hiraethhopeandhealing.com)

HH&H hosts healing retreats for adoptees, donor conceived people, late discovery adoptees, and NPEs. Five days and four nights of healing in a community, with a maximum of 30 attendees. They are hosted in private, upscale houses with carefully chosen facilitators who are experts in their fields, and healing sessions that will benefit everyone, no matter what stage of the journey you are in. 10 delicious meals, 6 workshops, time to relax, renew and refresh, and foster friendships, both old and new. Come join us and experience the safety of being among folks who understand you before they even know you. No other retreat exists like these!

Author notes: There are numerous sub-groups for several of these support groups and resources. New support groups continuously develop. Author belongs to several of the above groups. This list does not indicate endorsements or recommendations. You can try several, one, or all, and you can unfollow or leave any group at any time.

Acknowledgements

It took a village to write *Ancestry Discoveries*. Thank you, Raymond Gulzeth, my loving husband and best friend who said so many times, "Finish your book" when I should have been working. I am grateful for your love, your patience, your editing, listening, sense of humor and manuscript reviews. Ray, you were the glue that sometimes held me together. Thank you to Philip Landsman, for your continued love, support, listening ear and comic relief. You are smart, innovative, loving, and kind; it's in the genes. How did I get so lucky to have you as my son? Mary Cate Wooley, Rocco Mazza, and Kim Delmar, you are three of my oldest and dearest friends. Mary Cate, thank you for being my original beta reader and offering your support, encouragement, and constructive feedback. Nobody reads faster than you. Rocco, your constructive feedback and gushing, glowing, beta report meant more than I could ever put into words. Thank you, Kim Delmar for your continuous support not only of my book, but for beta reading, following my blog, offering feedback, and for the countless emails to Alexandra A. Barrie showing support, friendship and love. You all mean the world to me.

Howard Wells, thank you for being a patient, candid, gentle, honest, fun editor and new friend. Your suggestions were all wonderful. Thank you for being tolerant and maintaining a sense of humor reminding me to maintain mine, too. Thank you, Jennie Hefren, for "getting it." One conversation and you understood exactly what I needed and pointed me in the right direction.

Dr. Lisa Rapp-McCall, thank you for your encouragement on this project. You said three words to me when you edited my autism chapter, "You can write." You have no idea how those three words carried me through times when I thought of scrapping this project. Erin Cosentino, you are a rock star. With as busy as you are, with all you have to do managing support groups, online meetings, retreats, book clubs, etc., not to mention your own professional life and family, you were one of the first to return manuscript feedback. Your encouragement to "hurry up and finish" so you had another book for book club, still makes me smile when I think about it. Thank you, Patrick Callahan for your emails, feedback, and inspiration. Thank you, Alesia Weiss, another rock star supporting MPEs and working long hours, and Carole Wise, for your honest, invaluable feedback. I am so blessed to have you all as beta readers and supporters in my work. Jill Teitelman, your help, your encouragement, and your incredible writing have been an inspiration to me.

I owe my gratitude to several people behind the scenes. Thank you for being in my life Aunt Rosie, Aunt Charlene, Aunt Lori and Aunt Samantha, Lyndsey, Vic and Anna, and of course, Bubbles. Bubbles, you encouraged me all the way through the manuscript and helped me cope through the trauma just by being you, a kind, compassionate human being who I am proud to call my favorite sister, "your only sister, for now." I send a special thank you to my niece Lynn Alice. Our hours of laughter along with your listening without judgment helped me to keep connected to the love I came from. Lynn Alice, you will always be my "sister."

Barbara Kerr, there are no words to say thank you to you. You were with me from the outset offering guidance and sage advice on any writing project I decided to undertake including a research paper you were kind enough to edit. You helped me get over my fear as well as providing me with a direction when I was floundering and close to drowning in my apprehension.

Thank you for initial edits and feedback, Tom Rolston and Rachael Stout. Thank you Pastor Joe Santucci for your continued support. Your compassionate listening ears are a literal Godsend. Thank you Mark Gassman for your emails of encouragement.

I am forever grateful for all of the individuals I have met as a result of this DNA discovery. I never would have met any one of you if this did not happen to me.

About the Author

 Annette L Becklund is a therapist for over twenty years, specializing in Developmental Disabilities, a Mental Health Consultant, and workshop facilitator. Originally from New Jersey, she is a person who found out her dad was not her biological father. Annette is an NPE (Not Parent Expected) woman who is a professional member of The MPE Counseling Collective, and a member of several support groups with approximately 10,000 members. Annette and her colleagues published a professional study in the *Journal of Integrative Medicine*, published an article on NPEs in *In Focus*, a magazine for therapists in Florida, and has spoken on Ancestry Discoveries and related treatment. She facilitates a Facebook page on Ancestry Discoveries and has been a guest on a podcast on the same topic. Annette self-published *Warren is Wonderful*, a children's book for children with autism. She loves spending time with her husband Ray, a talented artist, her three pups Abbie, Zeva, and Rafiki, and cat, Spirit.

For more info: AnnetteLBecklund.com and

AncestryDiscoveries.com.